STORIES FOR BOYS who DARE to be DIFFERENT

A GUIDED JOURNAL

First published in Great Britain in 2020 by

Quercus Editions Ltd
Carmelite House
50 Victoria Embankment
London
EC4Y 0DZ

An Hachette UK company

A CIP catalogue record for this book is available
from the British Library

HB ISBN 978 1 529407 389

Every effort has been made to contact copyright
holders. However, the publishers will be glad
to rectify in future editions any inadvertent
omissions brought to their attention.

10 9 8 7 6 5 4 3 2 1

Inside design and illustrations by Sarah Greeno
Portrait illustrations by Quinton Winter
Printed and bound in China

STORIES FOR BOYS WHO DARE TO BE DIFFERENT

A GUIDED JOURNAL

Ben Brooks

PORTRAIT ILLUSTRATIONS BY QUINTON WINTER

Quercus

INTRODUCTION

Some boys are loud, some boys are quiet. Some design cars and some design dresses. Some have spent their lives fighting for the planet, while others have fought for the lives of those less fortunate than themselves.

All boys are different, but every single one has the potential to make the world a better place. Including you.

I wrote *Stories for Boys Who Dare To Be Different* to show there is no one way of being a boy. You do not have to play a certain sport, speak a certain way, or ever be afraid of looking silly, strange or stupid. You do not have to do anything, other than be kind to the people around you, occasionally make your bed and search for a passion that will keep you excited for years to come. In the words of Ryan Hreljac, who started his clean water charity at the age of six, 'the world is like a great big puzzle and we all have to figure out where our puzzle piece fits'.

The ideas and activities in this journal are there to help spark your ideas, dreams and ambitions, and get you thinking about a few things you might not have thought about before. They are there to be done wherever you want, whenever you want, and in whichever order you feel like. Your responses can be kept private, shared with friends or even broadcast to the world.

I hope this book can help you on the road to understanding how you think and how you feel. I hope it will be fun too. And I hope it will help you work out where to put your puzzle piece.

THINK OF YOUR BIGGEST FEAR. NOW PLOT A FILM IN WHICH THE MAIN CHARACTER OVERCOMES THAT FEAR. HOW DO THEY SUCCEED?

TITLE: ....
....
....

CHARACTERS: ....
....
....
....
....
....
....

PLOT: ....

....

....

....

....

....

....

....

....

....

....

....

....

After Achmat Hassiem lost his leg to a shark while saving his brother, he became a Paralympic athlete. The audience at his first Olympics shouted, 'Shark boy! Shark boy!' as he entered the arena.

WHAT NICKNAME WOULD YOU LIKE AN AUDIENCE TO CHANT FOR YOU? WHY HAVE YOU CHOSEN THAT NICKNAME?

<<<<<<<<<<<<<<<<<<<<<<<<

IF YOU COULD SPEAK TO ANY ONE PERSON FROM HISTORY, WHAT WOULD YOU ASK THEM AND WHY?

<<<<<<<<<<<<<<<<<<<<<<<<

WRITE DOWN THREE QUALITIES YOU THINK PEOPLE NORMALLY ASSOCIATE WITH GIRLS.

1. ....
....
....
....

2. ....
....
....
....

3. ....
....
....
....

NOW WRITE DOWN THREE REASONS WHY IT WOULD BE GOOD FOR YOU TO HAVE THOSE QUALITIES TOO.

1. ....

....

....

....

2. ....

....

....

....

3. ....

....

....

....

Christian McPhilamy grew his hair for two years so that he could donate it to kids who'd lost theirs to cancer. Although other children in his class bullied him, Christian knew how much happiness his hair would eventually bring to others.

THINK OF SOMETHING YOU'VE ALWAYS WANTED TO DO BUT NEVER HAVE, AND WRITE A SHORT NEWSPAPER ARTICLE FROM THE POINT OF VIEW OF A REPORTER WHO'S JUST SEEN YOU DO IT.

IMAGINE YOURSELF FROM A YEAR AGO. HELLO, SMALLER YOU!

WHAT WOULD YOU LIKE TO TELL HIM ABOUT YOUR LIFE RIGHT NOW?

....

....

....

....

....

....

....

Ryan Hreljac started a charity when he was just six years old, which he is still running today as an adult. Ryan's Well Foundation has helped almost a million people living in Africa to get access to clean water.

MAKE A THREE-YEAR PLAN FOR A CHARITY THAT WILL BE DEDICATED TO A CAUSE YOU'RE PASSIONATE ABOUT.

NAME OF CHARITY: ....

....

AIM: ....

....

....

GOALS FOR YEAR 1:   GOALS FOR YEAR 2:   GOALS FOR YEAR 3:

....

....

....

....

ARE YOU OK?

 IF YES, DRAW A THUMBS UP.

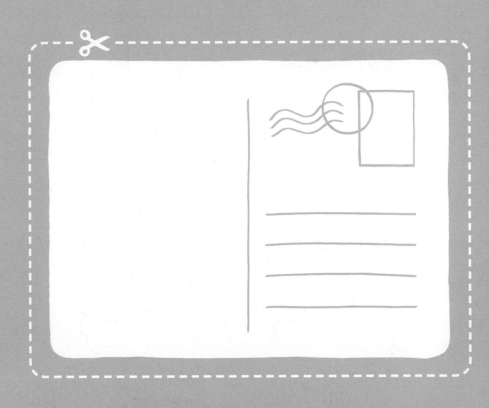

IF NOT, CUT OUT THIS POSTCARD, WRITE DOWN WHAT'S
BOTHERING YOU, AND GIVE IT TO SOMEONE YOU TRUST.

John Lennon and Yoko Ono once stayed in bed for two weeks to protest against war. They wanted to prove that there are many ways to fight for change in the world.

CREATE YOUR OWN NEW FORM OF PROTEST TO DRAW ATTENTION TO AN ISSUE THAT MEANS SOMETHING TO YOU.

ISSUE I WANT TO RAISE AWARENESS OF: ....

....

....

HOW I WANT TO DO IT: ....

....

....

....

....

....

....

DRAW A POSTER THAT LETS PEOPLE IN YOUR CLASS KNOW THAT THEY CAN TALK TO YOU IF THEY EVER NEED HELP.

IF YOU'RE FEELING BRAVE, PUT IT UP.

IMAGINE WRITING A BOOK FOR YOUNG CHILDREN ABOUT A CERTAIN FEELING.

Now make up a name for the main character based on this feeling. Draw how they look below.

FEELING: ....

....

THEIR NAME: ....

....

....

THEIR PERSONALITY: ....

....

....

....

....

....

....

....

....

IMAGINE THAT AN ALIEN IS TRAVELLING THROUGH THE UNIVERSE, HANDING OUT SURVEYS TO GATHER INFORMATION ABOUT LIFE ON OTHER PLANETS.

He's given you the survey
about the people of planet Earth
to complete. What would you write?

NAME OF INHABITANTS: HUMANS

STRANGEST THING THEY DO:

....

....

GREATEST THING THEY DO:

....

....

WHAT THEY DO WHEN THEY'RE SAD:

....

....

WHAT THEY DO WHEN THEY'RE HAPPY:

....

....

David Attenborough has devoted his life to travelling the globe and capturing the wonders of nature on film for us all to see. He's very worried about how we are destroying our planet and its wildlife, and once said, 'The question is, are we happy to suppose that our grandchildren may never be able to see an elephant except in a picture book?'

WHICH PART OF NATURE WOULD YOU BE SADDEST TO LOSE AND WHY? DO SOME RESEARCH AND FIND THREE WAYS YOU MIGHT BE ABLE TO HELP.

THING YOU WOULD BE SADDEST TO LOSE:

....

WHY: ....

....

....

WAYS YOU CAN HELP:

1. ....

2. ....

3. ....

A FAMOUS ACTOR HAS JUST ACCEPTED THE ROLE OF YOU IN A THEATRE PLAY BASED ON YOUR LIFE.

He wants to know three of your habits and the reasons you think you have them, so that he can be the most convincing *you* possible.

Help him out!

HABIT: ....

....

WHY I DO IT: ....

....

....

HABIT: ....

....

WHY I DO IT: ....

....

....

HABIT: ....

....

WHY I DO IT: ....

....

....

Confucius gave out all sorts of wise advice in the form of sayings, like 'Wherever you go, go with all your heart' and 'Our greatest glory is not in never falling, but in rising every time we fall.'

COME UP WITH YOUR OWN SAYING THAT MIGHT HELP SOMEONE OUT IF THEY'RE FEELING LONELY.

WRITE A <u>POEM</u>.
DON'T MAKE IT
RHYME. IN FACT,
MAKE IT SOUND AS
<u>UN-POETIC</u> AS YOU
CAN, JUST AS LONG
AS YOU MEAN IT.

CREATE THE PLOT OF AN EXCITING DREAM THAT SOMEONE YOU CARE ABOUT WOULD ENJOY HAVING.

WRITE DOWN WHAT YOU THINK WOULD MAKE YOU HAPPY ...

TODAY:...............................

....

....

....

A WEEK FROM NOW: ....

....

....

....

A MONTH FROM NOW: . . . .

. . . .

. . . .

. . . .

A YEAR FROM NOW: . . . .

. . . .

. . . .

. . . .

TEN YEARS FROM NOW: . . . .

. . . .

. . . .

. . . .

DESCRIBE THE MOST BEAUTIFUL PLACE YOU'VE EVER SEEN AND HOW YOU FELT WHILE YOU WERE THERE.

As a boy, James Earl Jones developed a stutter which was so bad he stopped speaking altogether. Eventually, with the help of poetry and acting, he learned to talk again and went on to become one of the most recognizable voices in the world.

THINK OF THREE WAYS YOU COULD COMMUNICATE YOUR FEELINGS TO A FRIEND WITHOUT USING WORDS.

1. ....
....
....

2. ....
....
....

3. ....
....
....

LIST FIVE THINGS THAT YOU HAVE SEEN MAKE PEOPLE CRY HAPPY TEARS.

1. ....

....

2. ....

....

3. ....

....

4. ....

....

5. ....

....

IF YOU COULD LIVE INSIDE ONE BOOK, WHICH BOOK WOULD IT BE AND WHY?

BOOK TITLE: ....

....

....

....

WHY: ....

....

....

....

....

....

....

....

....

....

....

DESIGN A MENU FOR A PERSON WHO'S BEEN FEELING A LITTLE SAD LATELY.

HOW WOULD YOU CHEER THEM UP WITH FOOD?

STARTER

~

....

MAIN COURSE

~

....

DESSERT

~

....

DRINKS

~

....

'WALDEINSAMKEIT'
IS A GERMAN
WORD WHICH
MEANS 'THE
FEELING OF
BEING ALONE
IN A WOOD'.

'SAUDADE' IS A PORTUGESE WORD THAT CONTAINS THE FEELING OF LONGING FOR SOMEONE OR SOMETHING THAT IS GONE.

Come up with two of your own words to describe a mood or an emotion that doesn't yet have a name in English:

WORD: ....

DEFINITION: ....

....

WORD: ....

DEFINITION: ....

....

IMAGINE THAT
HUMANS STOPPED
HAVING ANY
FEELINGS TOMORROW.
NO ONE FEELS HAPPY
OR SAD OR AFRAID
OR JEALOUS.

LIST THREE THINGS THAT MIGHT CHANGE WHICH WOULD MAKE THE WORLD WORSE.

1. ....
....
....
....

2. ....
....
....
....

3. ....
....
....
....

Patch Adams wanted to spread as much happiness through the world as possible. He became a clown and a doctor, and started his own hospital to make patients better but happier too.

ADD YOUR OWN SUGGESTIONS TO HIS LIST OF WAYS TO DO THIS.

1. BE SILLY IN PUBLIC.

2. WEAR FUNNY CLOTHES.

3. BE FRIENDLY TO EVERYONE YOU MEET.

4.

5.

6.

7.

8.

9.

10.

11.

12.

IMAGINE THAT THE BOY OPPOSITE IS YOU. DRAW TATTOOS ON HIM TO SHOW HOW HE THINKS AND FEELS.

MAYBE A LION TO SHOW HE'S ANGRY, OR A RAINCLOUD TO SHOW HE'S FEELING DOWN.

Eugene Cernan was an astronaut and the last man to walk on the moon. When he was there, he wrote his daughter's name in the dust, where it will stay for 50,000 years.

WHAT WOULD YOU WRITE ON THE MOON?

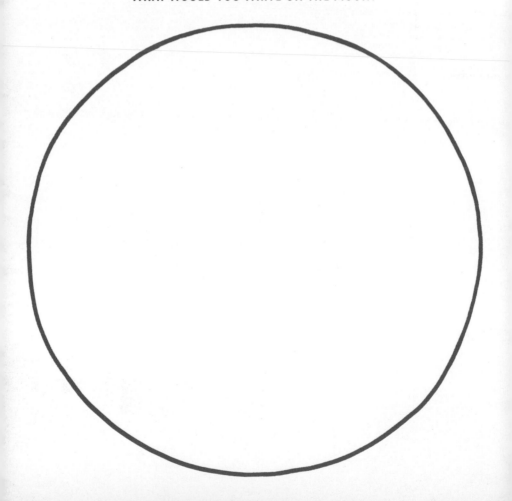

THINK OF ONE OF YOUR FAVOURITE SONGS AND REWRITE THE LYRICS OF THE CHORUS SO THAT THEY REFLECT YOUR LIFE.

YOU'RE PUT IN CHARGE OF YOUR COUNTRY FOR ONE DAY AND ARE ALLOWED TO PASS THREE LAWS.

WHICH THREE LAWS WOULD YOU PASS, AND WHY?

1. ....
....
....
....

2. ....
....
....
....

3. ....
....
....
....

Again and again, the footballer Lionel Messi has turned down vast sums of money to leave his club, Barcelona. The team looked after him when he was a boy with a growth hormone disorder and he's vowed to remain loyal to them throughout his career.

ON THE BACK OF THIS FOOTBALL SHIRT, LIST THE QUALITIES THAT MIGHT MAKE SOMEONE A GREAT FOOTBALL PLAYER.

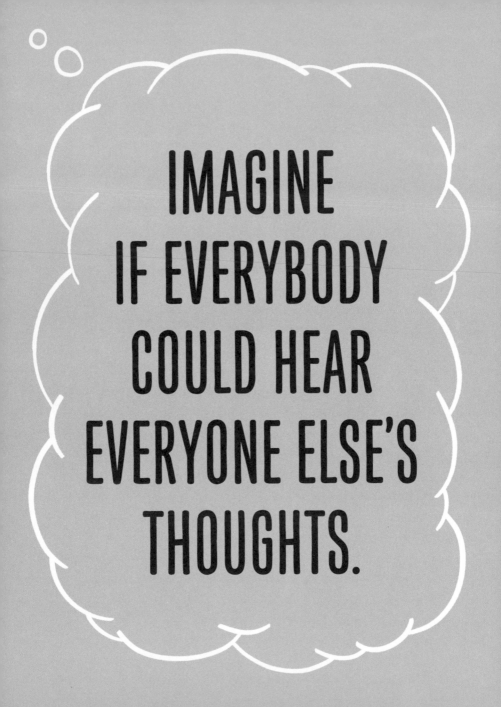

WOULD THIS BE A GOOD OR A BAD THING?

....

....

....

WHAT WOULD CHANGE?

....

....

....

WOULD YOU TRY TO THINK DIFFERENTLY?

....

....

....

Living in a country that had been occupied by the British, Gandhi taught his people to win back their independence using the idea of Satyagraha, or fighting violence with peace.

GANDHI ONCE SAID, 'AN EYE FOR AN EYE MAKES THE WHOLE WORLD BLIND.' DRAW A SCENE THAT ILLUSTRATES THIS.

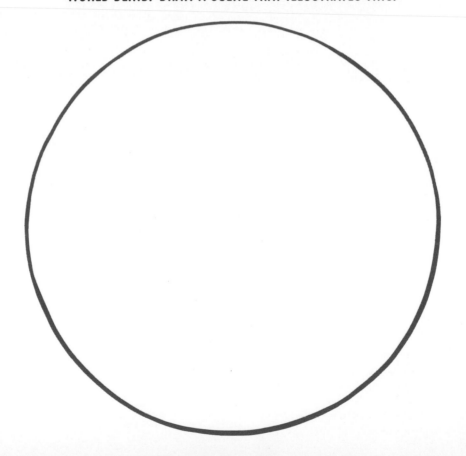

IMAGINE YOU COULD TRAVEL BACK TO MEDIEVAL TIMES.

WHAT'S ONE THING WE'VE LEARNED SINCE THEN THAT YOU WOULD TEACH TO THE PEOPLE OF THE MIDDLE AGES?

....

....

....

....

....

....

....

....

....

....

William Moulton Marston created Wonder Woman because he thought that there weren't enough strong female characters in comic books. He was inspired by famous feminists and the legendary tribes of fierce Amazon warriors.

DESIGN A SUPERHERO WITH QUALITIES THAT HAVE NEVER BEEN SEEN IN COMIC BOOKS OR MOVIES BEFORE.

LIST YOUR THREE LEAST FAVOURITE FEELINGS AND THE BEST WAYS OF OVERCOMING THEM.

CRUMMY FEELING: ....

HOW I OVERCOME IT: ....

....

....

CRUMMY FEELING: ....

HOW I OVERCOME IT: ....

....

....

CRUMMY FEELING: ....

HOW I OVERCOME IT: ....

....

....

NOW LIST YOUR THREE <u>FAVOURITE</u> FEELINGS AND THE THREE BEST WAYS OF <u>SPARKING</u> THEM.

FAVOURITE FEELING: ....

HOW I SPARK IT: ....

....

....

FAVOURITE FEELING: ....

HOW I SPARK IT: ....

....

....

FAVOURITE FEELING: ....

HOW I SPARK IT: ....

....

....

When Dan Kraus realized there was no service to help people whose cats had got stuck up trees, he knew he had to create one. He has since rescued over a thousand cats.

DESIGN AN ADVERT FOR A SERVICE YOU COULD PROVIDE TO YOUR LOCAL COMMUNITY.

YOU GET TO TEACH ONE LESSON ABOUT A PERSON TO A CLASS OF CHILDREN.

WHICH PERSON WOULD YOU MOST LIKE TO TEACH THEM ABOUT? WRITE A LESSON PLAN.

TITLE OF THE LESSON:

WHO WE'LL LEARN ABOUT:

WHAT WE CAN LEARN FROM THEIR STORY:

HOMEWORK:

WHAT IS THE HARDEST THING YOU'VE EVER HAD TO DO?

HOW

WOULD YOU

DEFINE THE WORD 'FAMILY'?

WHO MAKES UP YOUR FAMILY?

CAN YOU REMEMBER A DREAM THAT LEFT YOU FEELING HAPPY?

Bill Gates started Microsoft and went on to become the richest man in the world, though he no longer holds that title because he's given so much of his money away to charity.

IF YOU WON THE LOTTERY, WHAT WOULD YOU DO WITH THE MONEY?

WRITE A RESPONSE TO THESE WORDS OF MARTIN LUTHER KING:

'Every man must decide whether he will walk in the light of creative altruism or in the darkness of destructive selfishness. This is the judgement. Life's most urgent question is, what are you doing for others?'

PICK ONE OF THE MOST IMPORTANT OR EXCITING DAYS IN YOUR LIFE – IT COULD BE YOUR FIRST DAY AT SECONDARY SCHOOL, THE DAY A SIBLING WAS BORN OR THE DAY YOU WON A COMPETITION – AND WRITE THE SCRIPT FOR A SHORT PLAY BASED ON IT.

After his plane crashed during the Second World War, Roald Dahl found that people wanted him to write stories about his experiences. Instead, he wrote about chocolate factories and big, friendly giants. 'Those who don't believe in magic will never find it,' Roald said.

THE WRITER ROALD DAHL WAS NAMED AFTER THE EXPLORER ROALD AMUNDSEN. WRITE DOWN SOME NAMES BASED ON PEOPLE FROM HISTORY THAT YOU WOULD GIVE TO PEOPLE WHO WERE …

KIND: ....

....

....

QUIET: ....

....

....

BRAVE: ....

....

....

IF YOU HAD THE
ENTIRE PLANET
TO YOURSELF FOR
ONE DAY, WHAT
WOULD YOU SPEND
IT DOING?

PLAN A BEAUTIFUL GARDEN FILLED WITH POSSIBILITIES FOR ADVENTURE TO SPEND THE SUMMER IN.

Don McPherson went from being an American football player to travelling his country teaching boys to treat girls with respect and make sure they feel safe at all times.

ASK A GIRL YOU KNOW TO TELL YOU TWO WAYS THAT SHE THINKS SHE IS TREATED DIFFERENTLY FROM BOYS.

1. ....

....

2. ....

....

NOW WRITE DOWN TWO WAYS IN WHICH YOU COULD TRY TO HELP GET RID OF THOSE DIFFERENCES.

1. ....

....

2. ....

....

WRITE A SHORT SPEECH THAT YOU MIGHT WANT TO GIVE TO STOP SOMEONE BULLYING ANOTHER PERSON.

Galileo Galilei trained himself to grind lenses so he could make his
very own telescope, capable of seeing deep into the night sky.

CONNECT THE STARS IN THIS CHART INTO YOUR OWN CONSTELLATION AND GIVE IT A NAME. THEN, TONIGHT, LOOK UP AT THE SKY AND SEE IF YOU CAN SPOT IT.

NAME: ....

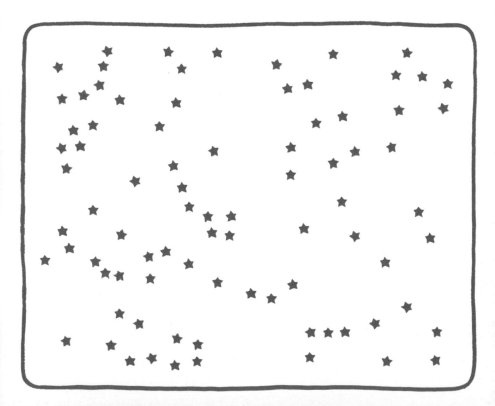

Grayson Perry has channelled his imagination and creativity into amazing ceramic designs that have earned him countless awards.

DESIGN YOUR OWN POT WITH SCENES OR TEXT THAT REFLECT YOUR LIFE.

IF YOU COULD HELP ANYONE IN THE WORLD, <u>WHO</u> WOULD YOU HELP, <u>HOW</u> WOULD YOU HELP THEM AND WHY?

During the Second World War, members of the White Rose movement scrawled graffiti across the walls of southern Germany to let the people know the truth about what was going on in their country.

DESIGN A PIECE OF GRAFFITI ON THIS WALL AIMED AT PROMOTING EQUALITY.

CUT OUT AND STICK IN THE SPACE BELOW
A PHOTO OF SOMEONE YOU ADMIRE.

Describe how you think they might have felt in
the moment the camera captured them.

WRITE AN APOLOGY FOR SOMETHING YOU NEVER HAD THE CHANCE TO APOLOGIZE FOR.

Ken Yeang thinks that the most important thing about a building is that it makes people happy. His buildings combine light and nature to make harmonious homes.

DESIGN A HOUSE THAT YOU THINK WOULD BRING JOY TO PEOPLE.

WRITE DOWN THREE WAYS OF SHOWING SOMEONE YOU LIKE THEM WITHOUT SAYING SO.

PUT YOUR WORDS INTO PRACTICE AND TICK
EACH ONE OFF WHEN YOU HAVE DONE IT.

1. ....

....

....

....

2. ....

....

....

....

3. ....

....

....

....

Christopher Paolini was just fifteen years old when he started work on his epic novel about dragons, *Eragon*.

DRAW THE COVER FOR A BOOK YOU HOPE TO WRITE.

WRITE DOWN THE FUNNIEST THING YOU'VE EVER ...

HEARD: ....

....

....

....

SEEN: ....

....

....

....

DONE: ....

....

....

....

At the start of his wonderful hip-hop career, Frank Ocean wasn't sure how the world might respond to him being gay. But when he came out he found that everyone loved him more than ever.

WHAT ONE THING HAVE YOU BEEN AFRAID TO TELL THE PEOPLE AROUND YOU ABOUT YOURSELF?

HOW DO YOU THINK THEY MIGHT REACT IF YOU DID?

CHOOSE THREE WEBSITE URLS THAT WOULD BEST DESCRIBE YOU AND YOUR FRIENDS.

YOUR NAME: ....

....

WEBSITE: WWW. ....

.... .COM

YOUR NAME: ....
....

WEBSITE: WWW. ....
.... .COM

YOUR NAME: ....
....

WEBSITE: WWW. ....
.... .COM

In 2009 Barack Obama became the first black president of the United States of America. It was a great leap forward that filled many people with hope.

WRITE A SHORT SPEECH THAT YOU WOULD DELIVER TO YOUR COUNTRY AFTER BEING MADE LEADER.

What hopes would you have for the future?
What promises would you make to the people of your country?

While he was at school, John Green was inspired by the books of Michael Chabon, Toni Morrison and J. D. Salinger. He turned his experiences of boarding school into his own novel for teenagers, *The Fault in Our Stars*, which went on to be a bestseller around the world.

WRITE A REPORT ABOUT YOUR FAVOURITE BOOK.

TITLE: ....

PLOT: ....

....

....

WHY I LOVE IT: ....

....

....

WHICH CHARACTER I MOST RELATE TO AND WHY: ....

....

....

WHAT'S THE SMALLEST THING ANYONE EVER DID FOR YOU THAT STILL MADE YOU VERY HAPPY?

Try doing that small thing for someone else.

Taika Waititi loved comic books as a boy but he could never see Maori people like himself in them. This drove him to tell his own stories in movies that he wrote and directed. People loved the films so much that he was asked to direct movies for Marvel, and now he has created his own comic book universe too.

DRAW AND WRITE A COMIC STRIP IN WHICH YOU'RE A HERO, HELPING SOMEONE YOU KNOW TO OVERCOME ONE OF THEIR FEARS.

WHEN WAS THE LAST TIME YOU CRIED? WHERE WERE YOU AND WHAT HAD UPSET YOU?

Trevor Noah has turned the pain of his childhood into comedy enjoyed by millions of people. He once said, 'If you laugh with somebody, then you know you share something.'

TRY WRITING A JOKE THAT COULD HELP YOU SHARE SOMETHING IN YOUR LIFE WITH OTHER PEOPLE.

WHAT WORRIES YOU MORE THAN ANYTHING ELSE?

WRITE IT DOWN HERE, THEN TELL SOMEONE YOU TRUST
AND SEE IF THEY HAVE ANY IDEAS THAT COULD HELP.

....

....

....

....

....

....

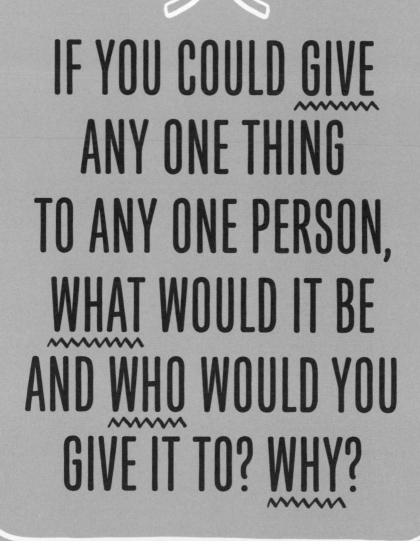

IF YOU COULD GIVE ANY ONE THING TO ANY ONE PERSON, WHAT WOULD IT BE AND WHO WOULD YOU GIVE IT TO? WHY?

WHAT: ....

....

....

WHO: ....

....

....

WHY: ....

....

....

Daniel Radcliffe's life changed for ever when he took on the role of Harry Potter. By playing the boy wizard in films, he learned to gain the confidence he'd never felt in real life.

IF YOU COULD PLAY ANY CHARACTER IN A FILM, WHICH CHARACTER WOULD YOU PLAY AND HOW WOULD PLAYING THAT CHARACTER HELP YOU?

WHICH FOUR THINGS DO YOU THINK ARE THE MOST IMPORTANT PARTS OF A HAPPY LIFE?

1. ....

....

2. ....

....

....

....

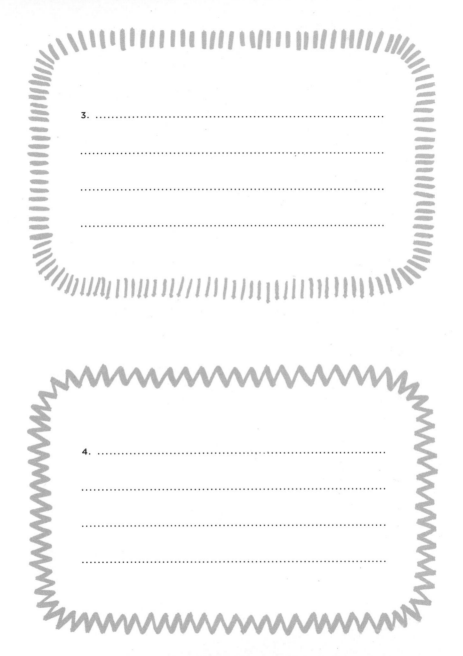

3. ....
....
....
....

4. ....
....
....
....

DESIGN A 'WANTED' POSTER FOR SOMETHING YOU THINK THE WORLD IS MISSING.

IT COULD BE LOVE, PATIENCE OR EVEN A TYPE OF PIZZA THAT HASN'T BEEN INVENTED YET.

WANTED

Steve Irwin devoted his life to showing the public that wild animals like crocodiles aren't scary beasts, but beautiful creatures that deserve to be protected.

WHAT IDEA WOULD YOU MOST LIKE TO CHANGE PEOPLE'S MINDS ABOUT?

WHAT ONE THING COULD YOU DO TOMORROW TO MAKE SOMEONE'S LIFE A LITTLE EASIER?

CHOOSE <u>THREE</u>
THINGS THAT YOU
THINK A <u>GOOD ROLE</u>
<u>MODEL</u> SHOULD
HAVE AND SPEND
A WEEK TRYING TO
<u>EMBODY</u> THEM.

QUALITY: ....

HOW I EMBODIED IT: ....

....

....

QUALITY: ....

HOW I EMBODIED IT: ....

....

....

QUALITY: ....

HOW I EMBODIED IT: ....

....

....

BEN BROOKS

was born in 1992 and lives in Berlin.
He is the author of several books,
including *Grow Up* and *Lolito*, which won
the Somerset Maugham Award in 2015.
He is the author of the international bestseller
Stories for Boys Who Dare To Be Different.

QUINTON WINTER

is a British illustrator, artist and colourist.
He has worked for many clients including
the *Guardian* newspaper, Walker Books,
Gogglebox, *2000AD*, Vertigo Comics,
Mojo and the BBC. He is the illustrator
of the international bestseller
Stories for Boys Who Dare To Be Different.

nicola yoon

INTERIOR ILLUSTRATIONS BY DAVID YOON

CORGI BOOKS

UK | USA | Canada | Ireland | Australia
India | New Zealand | South Africa

Corgi Books is part of the Penguin Random House group of companies
whose addresses can be found at global.penguinrandomhouse.com.

www.penguin.co.uk   www.puffin.co.uk   www.ladybird.co.uk

Penguin
Random House
UK

First published 2015
This edition published 2017

001

alloyentertainment

alloyentertainment.com

Typeset in Garamond
Printed in Great Britain by Clays Ltd, St Ives plc

A CIP catalogue record for this book is available from the British Library

ISBN: 978-0-552-57648-2

All correspondence to:
Corgi Books, Penguin Random House Children's
80 Strand, London WC2R ORL

To my husband, David Yoon, who showed me my heart.

And to my smart, beautiful daughter, Penny,
who made it bigger.

THE WHITE ROOM

I'VE READ MANY more books than you. It doesn't matter how many you've read. I've read more. Believe me. I've had the time.

In my white room, against my white walls, on my glistening white bookshelves, book spines provide the only color. The books are all brand-new hardcovers—no germy secondhand softcovers for me. They come to me from Outside, decontaminated and vacuum-sealed in plastic wrap. I would like to see the machine that does this. I imagine each book traveling on a white conveyor belt toward rectangular white stations where robotic white arms dust, scrape, spray, and otherwise sterilize it until it's finally deemed clean enough to come to me. When a new book arrives, my first task is to remove the wrapping, a process that involves scissors and more than one broken nail. My second task is to write my name on the inside front cover.

PROPERTY OF: *Madeline Whittier*

I don't know why I do this. There's no one else here except my mother, who never reads, and my nurse, Carla, who has no time to read because she spends all her time watching me breathe. I rarely have visitors, and so there's no one to lend my books to. There's no one who needs reminding that the forgotten book on his or her shelf belongs to me.

REWARD IF FOUND (Check all that apply):

This is the section that takes me the longest time, and I vary it with each book. Sometimes the rewards are fanciful:

- Picnic with me (Madeline) in a pollen-filled field of poppies, lilies, and endless man-in-the-moon marigolds under a clear blue summer sky.
- Drink tea with me (Madeline) in a lighthouse in the middle of the Atlantic Ocean in the middle of a hurricane.
- Snorkel with me (Madeline) off Molokini to spot the Hawaiian state fish— the humuhumunukunukuapuaa.

Sometimes the rewards are not so fanciful:

- A visit with me (Madeline) to a used bookstore.
- A walk outside with me (Madeline), just down the block and back.
- A short conversation with me (Madeline), discussing anything you want, on my white couch, in my white bedroom.

Sometimes the reward is just:

- Me (Madeline).

SCID ROW

MY DISEASE IS as rare as it is famous. It's a form of Severe Combined Immunodeficiency, but you know it as "bubble baby disease."

Basically, I'm allergic to the world. Anything can trigger a bout of sickness. It could be the chemicals in the cleaner used to wipe the table that I just touched. It could be someone's perfume. It could be the exotic spice in the food I just ate. It could be one, or all, or none of these things, or something else entirely. No one knows the triggers, but everyone knows the consequences. According to my mom I almost died as an infant. And so I stay on SCID row. I don't leave my house, have not left my house in seventeen years.

DAILY
HEALTH
LOG

Madeline Whittier
PATIENT NAME

May 2
DATE

Dr. Pauline Whittier
CARETAKER

0002921

4

BREATHS PER MINUTE

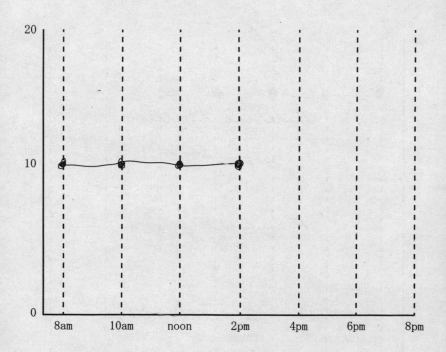

0002921

ROOM TEMPERATURE

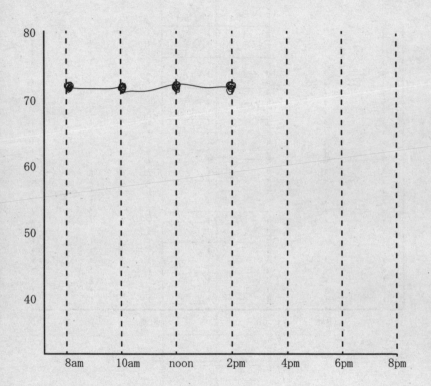

0002921

AIR FILTER STATUS

8am	OK
9am	OK
10am	OK
11am	OK
12pm	OK
1pm	OK
2pm	OK
3pm	
4pm	
5pm	
6pm	
7pm	
8pm	

0002921

7

BRTHDAE UISH

"MOVIE NIGHT OR Honor Pictionary or Book Club?" my mom asks while inflating a blood pressure cuff around my arm. She doesn't mention her favorite of all our post-dinner activities—Phonetic Scrabble. I look up to see that her eyes are already laughing at me.

"Phonetic," I say.

She stops inflating the cuff. Ordinarily Carla, my full-time nurse, would be taking my blood pressure and filling out my daily health log, but my mom's given her the day off. It's my birthday and we always spend the day together, just the two of us.

She puts on her stethoscope so that she can listen to my heartbeat. Her smile fades and is replaced by her more serious doctor's face. This is the face her patients most often see—slightly distant, professional, and concerned. I wonder if they find it comforting.

Impulsively I give her a quick kiss on the forehead to remind her that it's just me, her favorite patient, her daughter.

She opens her eyes, smiles, and caresses my cheek. I guess if you're going to be born with an illness that requires constant care, then it's good to have your mom as your doctor.

A few seconds later she gives me her best I'm-the-doctor-and-I'm-afraid-I-have-some-bad-news-for-you face. "It's your big day. Why don't we play something you have an actual chance of winning? Honor Pictionary?"

Since regular Pictionary can't really be played with two people, we invented Honor Pictionary. One person draws and the other person is on her *honor* to make her best guess. If you guess correctly, the other person scores.

I narrow my eyes at her. "We're playing Phonetic, and I'm winning this time," I say confidently, though I have no chance of winning. In all our years of playing Phonetic Scrabble, or Fonetik Skrabbl, I've never beaten her at it. The last time we played I came close. But then she devastated me on the final word, playing *JEENZ* on a triple word score.

"OK." She shakes her head with mock pity. "Anything you want." She closes her laughing eyes to listen to the stethoscope.

We spend the rest of the morning baking my traditional birthday cake of vanilla sponge with vanilla cream frosting. After it's cooled, I apply an unreasonably thin layer of frosting, just enough to cover the cake. We are, both of us, cake people, not frosting people. For decoration, I draw eighteen frosted daisies with white petals and a white center across the top. On the sides I fashion draped white curtains.

"Perfect." My mom peers over my shoulders as I finish up. "Just like you."

I turn to face her. She's smiling a wide, proud smile at me, but her eyes are bright with tears.

"You. Are. Tragic," I say, and squirt a dollop of frosting on her nose, which only makes her laugh and cry some more. Really, she's not usually this emotional, but something about my birthday always makes her both weepy and joyful at the same time. And if she's weepy and joyful, then I'm weepy and joyful, too.

"I know," she says, throwing her hands helplessly up in the air. "I'm totally pathetic." She pulls me into a hug and squeezes. Frosting gets into my hair.

My birthday is the one day of the year that we're both most acutely aware of my illness. It's the acknowledging of the passage of time that does it. Another whole year of being sick, no hope for a cure on the horizon. Another year of missing all the normal teenagery things—learner's permit, first kiss, prom, first heartbreak, first fender bender. Another year of my mom doing nothing but working and taking care of me. Every other day these omissions are easy—easier, at least—to ignore.

This year is a little harder than the previous. Maybe it's because I'm eighteen now. Technically, I'm an adult. I should be leaving home, going off to college. My mom should be dreading empty-nest syndrome. But because of SCID, I'm not going anywhere.

Later, after dinner, she gives me a beautiful set of watercolor pencils that had been on my wish list for months. We go into the living room and sit cross-legged in front of the coffee table. This is also part of our birthday ritual: She lights a single candle in the center of the cake. I close my eyes and make a wish. I blow the candle out.

"What did you wish for?" she asks as soon as I open my eyes.

Really there's only one thing to wish for—a magical cure that will allow me to run free outside like a wild animal. But I never make that wish because it's impossible. It's like wishing that mermaids and dragons and unicorns were real. Instead I wish for something more likely than a cure. Something less likely to make us both sad.

"World peace," I say.

Three slices of cake later, we begin a game of Fonetik. I do not win. I don't even come close.

She uses all seven letters and puts down POKALIP next to an S. POKALIPS.

"What's that?" I ask.

"Apocalypse," she says, eyes dancing.

"No, Mom. No way. I can't give that to you."

"Yes," is all she says.

"Mom, you need an extra A. No way."

"Pokalips," she says for effect, gesturing at the letters. "It totally works."

I shake my head.

"P O K A L I P S," she insists, slowly dragging out the word.

"Oh my God, you're relentless," I say, throwing my hands up. "OK, OK, I'll allow it."

"Yesssss." She pumps her fist and laughs at me and marks

11

down her now-insurmountable score. "You've never really understood this game," she says. "It's a game of persuasion."

I slice myself another piece of cake. "That was not persuasion," I say. "That was cheating."

"Same same," she says, and we both laugh.

"You can beat me at Honor Pictionary tomorrow," she says.

After I lose, we go to the couch and watch our favorite movie, *Young Frankenstein*. Watching it is also part of our birthday ritual. I put my head in her lap, and she strokes my hair, and we laugh at the same jokes in the same way that we've been laughing at them for years. All in all, not a bad way to spend your eighteenth birthday.

STAYS THE SAME

I'M READING ON my white couch when Carla comes in the next morning.

"*Feliz cumpleaños,*" she sings out.

I lower my book. "*Gracias.*"

"How was the birthday?" She begins unpacking her medical bag.

"We had fun."

"Vanilla cake and vanilla frosting?" she asks.

"Of course."

"*Young Frankenstein?*"

"Yes."

"And you lost at that game?" she asks.

"We're pretty predictable, huh?"

"Don't mind me," she says, laughing. "I'm just jealous of how sweet you and your mama are."

She picks up my health log from yesterday, quickly reviews my mom's measurements and adds a new sheet to the clipboard. "These days Rosa can't even be bothered to give me the time of day."

Rosa is Carla's seventeen-year-old daughter. According to Carla they were really close until hormones and boys took over. I can't imagine that happening to my mom and me.

Carla sits next to me on the couch, and I hold out my hand for the blood pressure cuff. Her eyes drop to my book.

"*Flowers for Algernon* again?" she asks. "Doesn't that book always make you cry?"

"One day it won't," I say. "I want to be sure to be reading it on that day."

She rolls her eyes at me and takes my hand.

It *is* kind of a flip answer, but then I wonder if it's true.

Maybe I'm holding out hope that one day, someday, things will change.

LIFE IS SHORT™
SPOILER REVIEWS BY MADELINE

FLOWERS FOR ALGERNON BY DANIEL KEYES
Spoiler alert: Algernon is a mouse. The mouse dies.

ALIEN INVASION, PART 2

I'M UP TO the part where Charlie realizes that the mouse's fate may be his own when I hear a loud rumbling noise outside. Immediately my mind goes to outer space. I picture a giant mother ship hovering in the skies above us.

The house trembles and my books vibrate on the shelves. A steady beeping joins the rumbling and I know what it is. A truck. Probably just lost, I tell myself, to stave off disappointment. Probably just made a wrong turn on their way to someplace else.

But then the engine cuts off. Doors open and close. A moment passes, and then another, and then a woman's voice sings out, "Welcome to our new home, everybody!"

Carla stares at me hard for a few seconds. I know what she's thinking.

It's happening again.

MADELINE'S DIARY

August 5

The family in the house next door moved away. ~~The~~ The boy cried. He hid in the garden and ate dirt whitill his mom found him but she didn't yell at him for eating it like she usually does. Outside is so quiet now. Last night I had a dream that they

didn't really move away.
They got kidnapped
by aliens. The aliens
didn't take me because
I'm sick and they only
wanted healthy people.
They took mommy and
carla away and the
family next door and I
was all alone.

I woke up crying
and mommy came and
stayed in bed with
me. I didn't tell her
what the dream was
about because it would
make her sad, but
I told Carla and
she gave me a hug.

THE WELCOME COMMITTEE

"CARLA," I SAY, "it won't be like last time." I'm not eight years old anymore.

"I want you to promise—" she begins, but I'm already at the window, sweeping the curtains aside.

I am not prepared for the bright California sun. I'm not prepared for the sight of it, high and blazing hot and white against the washed-out white sky. I am blind. But then the white haze over my vision begins to clear. Everything is haloed.

I see the truck and the silhouette of an older woman twirling—the mother. I see an older man at the back of the truck—the father. I see a girl maybe a little younger than me—the daughter.

Then I see him. He's tall, lean, and wearing all black: black T-shirt, black jeans, black sneakers, and a black knit cap that covers his hair completely. He's white with a pale honey tan and his face is starkly angular. He jumps down from his perch at the back of the truck and glides across the driveway, moving as if gravity affects him differently than it does the rest of us. He stops, cocks his head to one side, and stares up at his new house as if it were a puzzle.

After a few seconds he begins bouncing lightly on the balls of his feet. Suddenly he takes off at a sprint and runs literally six feet up the front wall. He grabs a windowsill and dangles from it for a second or two and then drops back down into a crouch.

"Nice, Olly," says his mother.

"Didn't I tell you to quit doing that stuff?" his father growls.

He ignores them both and remains in his crouch.

I press my open palm against the glass, breathless as if I'd done that crazy stunt myself. I look from him to the wall to the windowsill and back to him again. He's no longer crouched. He's staring up at me. Our eyes meet. Vaguely I wonder what he sees in my window—strange girl in white with wide staring eyes. He grins at me and his face is no longer stark, no longer severe. I try to smile back, but I'm so flustered that I frown at him instead.

MY WHITE BALLOON

THAT NIGHT, I dream that the house breathes with me. I exhale and the walls contract like a pinpricked balloon, crushing me as it deflates. I inhale and the walls expand. A single breath more and my life will finally, finally explode.

NEIGHBORHOOD WATCH

HIS MOM'S SCHEDULE

6:35 AM - Arrives on porch with a steaming cup of
something hot. Coffee?

6:36 AM - Stares off into empty lot across the way
while sipping her drink. Tea?

7:00 AM - Reenters the house.

7:15 AM - Back on porch. Kisses husband good-bye.
Watches as his car drives away.

9:30 AM - Gardens. Looks for, finds, and discards
cigarette butts.

1:00 PM - Leaves house in car. Errands?

5:00 PM - Pleads with Kara and Olly to begin chores
"before your father gets home."

KARA'S (SISTER) SCHEDULE

10:00 AM - Stomps outside wearing black boots and a
fuzzy brown bathrobe.

10:01 AM - Checks cell phone messages. She gets a lot of
messages.

10:06 AM - Smokes three cigarettes in the garden between
our two houses

10:20 AM - Digs a hole with the toe of her boots and
buries cigarette carcasses.
10:25 AM—5:00 PM - Texts or talks on the phone.
5:25 PM - Chores.

HIS DAD'S SCHEDULE
7:15 AM - Leaves for work.
6:00 PM - Arrives home from work.
6:20 PM - Sits on porch with drink #1.
6:30 PM - Reenters the house for dinner.
7:00 PM - Back on porch with drink #2.
7:25 PM - Drink #3.
7:45 PM - Yelling at family begins.
10:35 PM - Yelling at family subsides.

OLLY'S SCHEDULE
Unpredictable.

I SPY

HIS FAMILY CALLS him Olly. Well, his sister and his mom call him Olly. His dad calls him Oliver. He's the one I watch the most. His bedroom is on the second floor and almost directly across from mine and his blinds are almost always open.

Some mornings he sleeps in until noon. Others, he's gone from his room before I wake to begin my surveillance. Most mornings, though, he wakes at 9 A.M., climbs out of his bedroom, and makes his way, Spider-Man-style, to the roof using the siding. He stays up there for about an hour before swinging, legs first, back into his room. No matter how much I try, I haven't been able to see what he does when he's up there.

His room is empty but for a bed and a chest of drawers. A few boxes from the move remain unpacked and stacked by the doorway. There are no decorations except for a single poster for a movie called *Jump London*. I looked it up and it's about parkour, which is a kind of street gymnastics, which explains how he's able to do all the crazy stuff that he does. The more I watch, the more I want to know.

MENTEUSE

I'VE JUST SAT down at the dining table for dinner. My mom places a cloth napkin in my lap and fills my water glass and then Carla's. Friday night dinners are special in my house. Carla even stays late to eat with us instead of with her own family.

Everything at Friday Night Dinner is French. The napkins are white cloth embroidered with fleur-de-lis at the edges. The cutlery is antique French and ornate. We even have miniature silver *la tour Eiffel* salt and pepper shakers. Of course, we have to be careful with the menu because of my allergies, but my mom always makes her version of a cassoulet—a French stew with chicken, sausage, duck, and white beans. It was my dad's favorite dish before he died. The version that my mom cooks for me contains only white beans cooked in chicken broth.

"Madeline," my mom says, "Mr. Waterman tells me that you're late on your architecture assignment. Is everything all right, baby girl?"

I'm surprised by her question. I know I'm late, but since I've never been late before I guess I didn't realize that she was keeping track.

"Is the assignment too hard?" She frowns as she ladles cassoulet into my bowl. "Do you want me to find you a new tutor?"

"Oui, non, et non," I say in response to each question. "Everything's fine. I'll turn it in tomorrow, I promise. I just lost track of time."

She nods and begins slicing and buttering pieces of crusty French bread for me. I know she wants to ask something else. I even know what she wants to ask, but she's afraid of the answer.

"Is it the new neighbors?"

Carla gives me a sharp look. I've never lied to my mom. I've never had a reason and I don't think I know how to. But something tells me what I need to do.

"I've just been reading too much. You know how I get with a good book." I make my voice as reassuring as possible. I don't want her to worry. She has enough to worry about with me as it is.

How do you say "liar" in French?

"Not hungry?" my mom asks a few minutes later. She presses the back of her hand against my forehead.

"You don't have a fever." She lets her hand linger a moment longer.

I'm about to reassure her when the doorbell rings. This happens so infrequently that I don't know what to make of it.

The bell rings again.

My mom half rises from her chair.

Carla stands all the way up.

The bell sounds for a third time. I smile for no reason.

"Want me to get it, ma'am?" Carla asks.

My mom waves her off. "Stay here," she says to me.

Carla moves to stand behind me, her hands pressing down lightly on my shoulder. I know I should stay here. I know I'm expected to. Certainly I expect me to, but somehow, today, I just can't. I need to know who it is, even if it's just a wayward traveler.

Carla touches my upper arm. "Your mother said to stay here."

"But why? She's just being extra cautious. Besides, she won't let anyone past the air lock."

She relents, and I'm off down the hallway with her right behind me.

The air lock is a small sealed room surrounding the front door. It's airtight so that no potential hazards can leak into the main house when the front door is open. I press my ear against it. At first I can't hear anything over the air filters, but then I hear a voice.

"My mom sent a Bundt." The voice is deep and smooth and definitely amused. My brain is processing the word *Bundt*, trying to get an image of what it looks like before it dawns on me just who is at the door. Olly.

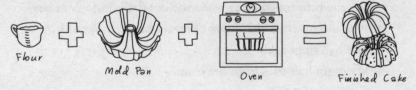

Flour   Mold Pan   Oven   Finished Cake

The Bundt Cake

"The thing about my mom's Bundts is that they are not very good. Terrible. Actually inedible, very nearly indestructible. Between you and me."

A new voice now. A girl's. His sister? "Every time we move she makes us bring one to the neighbor."

"Oh. Well. This is a surprise, isn't it? That's very nice. Please tell her thank you very much for me."

There's no chance that this Bundt cake has passed the proper inspections, and I can feel my mom trying to figure out how to tell them she can't take the cake without revealing the truth about me.

"I'm sorry, but I can't accept this."

There's a moment of shocked silence.

"So you want us to take it back?" Olly asks disbelievingly.

"Well, that's rude," Kara says. She sounds angry and resigned, as though she'd expected disappointment.

"I'm so sorry," my mom says again. "It's complicated. I'm really very sorry because this is so sweet of you and your mom. Please thank her for me."

"Is your daughter home?" Olly asks quite loudly, before she can close the door. "We're hoping she could show us around."

My heart speeds up and I can feel the pulse of it against my ribs. Did he just ask about me? No stranger has just dropped by to visit me before. Aside from my mom, Carla, and my tutors, the world barely knows I exist. I mean, I exist online. I have online friends and my Tumblr book reviews, but that's not the same as being a real person who can be visited by strange boys bearing Bundt cakes.

"I'm so sorry, but she can't. Welcome to the neighborhood, and thank you again."

The front door closes and I step back to wait for my mom. She has to remain in the air lock until the filters have a chance to purify the foreign air. A minute later she steps back into the house. She doesn't notice me right away. Instead she stands still, eyes closed with her head slightly bowed.

"I'm sorry," she says, without looking up.

"I'm OK, Mom. Don't worry."

For the thousandth time I realize anew how hard my disease is on her. It's the only world I've known, but before me she had my brother and my dad. She traveled and played soccer. She had a normal life that did not include being cloistered in a bubble for fourteen hours a day with her sick teenage daughter.

I hold her and let her hold me for a few more minutes. She's taking this disappointment much harder than I am.

"I'll make it up to you," she says.

"There's nothing to make up for."

"I love you, sweetie."

We drift back into the dining room and finish dinner quickly and, for the most part, silently. Carla leaves and my mom asks if I want to beat her at a game of Honor Pictionary, but I ask for a rain check. I'm not really in the mood.

Instead, I head upstairs imagining what a Bundt cake tastes like.

PIÈCE DE REJECTION

BACK IN MY room, I go immediately to my bedroom window. His dad is home from work and something's wrong because he's angry and getting angrier by the second. He grabs the Bundt cake from Kara and throws it hard at Olly, but Olly's too fast, too graceful. He dodges, and the cake falls to the ground.

Remarkably the Bundt seems unharmed, but the plate shatters against the driveway. This only makes his dad angrier.

"You clean that up. You clean that up right now." He slams into the house. His mom goes after him. Kara shakes her head at Olly and says something to him that makes his shoulders slump. Olly stands there looking at the cake for a few minutes. He disappears into the house and returns with a broom and dustpan. He takes his time, way longer than necessary, sweeping up the broken plate.

When he's done he climbs to the roof, taking the Bundt with him, and it's another hour before he swings back into his room.

I'm hiding in my usual spot behind the curtain when I suddenly no longer want to hide. I turn on the lights and go back to the window. I don't even bother to take a deep breath. It's not going to help. I pull the curtain aside to find that he's already there in his window, staring right at me. He doesn't smile. He doesn't wave. Instead, he reaches his arm overhead and pulls the blind closed.

SURVIVAL

"HOW LONG ARE you going to mope around the house?" Carla asks. "You've been like this all week."

"I'm not moping," I say, though I've been moping a little. Olly's rejection has made me feel like a little girl again. It reminded me why I stopped paying attention to the world before.

But trying to get back to my normal routine is hard when I can hear all the sounds of the outside world. I notice things that I paid very little attention to before. I hear the wind disturbing the trees. I hear birds gossiping in the mornings. I see the rectangles of sunlight that slip through my blinds and work their way across the room throughout the day. You can mark time by them. As much as I'm trying to keep the world out, it seems determined to come in.

"You've been reading the same five pages in that book for days now." She nods at my copy of *Lord of the Flies*.

"Well, it's a terrible book."

"I thought it was a classic."

"It's terrible. Most of the boys are awful and all they talk about is hunting and killing pigs. I've never been so hungry for bacon in my life."

She laughs, but it's halfhearted at best. She sits on the couch next to me and moves my legs into her lap. "Tell me," she says.

I put the book down and close my eyes. "I just want them to go away," I confess. "It was easier before."

"What was easier?"

"I don't know. Being me. Being sick."

She squeezes my leg. "You listen to me now. You're the strongest, bravest person I know. You better believe that."

"Carla, you don't have to—"

"Shush, listen to me. I've been thinking this over. I could see this new thing was weighing down on you, but I know you're going to be all right."

"I'm not so sure."

"That's OK. I can be sure for both of us. We've been together in this house for fifteen years, so I know what I'm talking about. When I first started with you I thought it was only a matter of time before depression would take you over. And there was that one summer when it came close, but it didn't happen. Every day you get up and learn something new. Every day you find something to be happy about. Every single day you have a smile for me. You worry more about your mother than you do about yourself."

I don't think Carla has ever said this many words all at once.

"My own Rosa," she continues, but then stops. She leans back and closes her eyes in the grip of some emotion I don't understand. "My Rosa could learn a thing or two from you. She has everything I could give her, but she thinks she has nothing."

I smile. Carla complains about her daughter, but I can tell she spoils her as much as she can.

She opens her eyes, and whatever was bothering her passes. "You see, there's that smile again." She pats my leg. "Life is hard, honey. Everyone finds a way."

LIFE IS SHORT™
SPOILER REVIEWS BY MADELINE

LORD OF THE FLIES BY WILLIAM GOLDING
Spoiler alert: Boys are savages.

FIRST CONTACT

TWO DAYS PASS and I've stopped moping. I'm getting better at ignoring the neighbors when I hear a ping coming from outside. I'm on my couch, still mired in *Lord of the Flies*. Mercifully, I'm close to finishing. Ralph is on the beach awaiting a violent death. I'm so eager for the book to end so that I can read something else, something happier, that I ignore the sound. A few minutes later there's another ping, louder this time. I put the book down and listen. Pings three, four, and five come in rapid succession. Something's hitting my window. Hail? I'm up and at my window before I can think better of it. I push the curtains aside.

Olly's window is wide open, the blinds are up, and the lights are off in his room. The indestructible Bundt is sitting on his windowsill wearing googly eyes that are staring right at me. The cake trembles and then tilts forward, as if contemplating the distance to the ground. It retreats and trembles some more. I'm trying to see Olly in his darkened room when the Bundt leaps from the sill and plunges to the ground.

I gasp. Did the cake just commit suicide? I crane my neck to see what's become of it, but it's too dark out.

Just then a spotlight illuminates the cake. Unbelievably, it's still intact. What is that thing made of? It's probably best that we didn't try to eat it.

The light goes out and I look up just in time to catch Olly's black-clad hand and flashlight retreat into the window. I stay for a few minutes, watching and waiting for him to come back, but he doesn't.

NIGHT TWO

I'M JUST SETTLING in to bed when the pings begin again. I am determined to ignore him, and I do. Whatever he wants I can't do. It's easier not to know.

I don't go to the window that night or the next.

NIGHT FOUR

I CAN'T STAND it. I peck out from the corner of my curtains.

The Bundt is sitting on the sill, Band-Aids and bandages covering half its body. Olly is nowhere to be found.

NIGHT FIVE

THE BUNDT IS sitting on a table next to the window. There's a martini glass filled with green liquid, a pack of cigarettes, and a pill bottle with a skull and crossbones label. Another suicide attempt?

Still no Olly.

NIGHT SIX

THE BUNDT IS lying on a white sheet. An upside-down plastic water bottle is attached to what looks like a coat hanger and is hanging above the cake. A string hangs from the bottle to the Bundt like an IV. Olly appears wearing a white jacket and stethoscope. He's frowning down at the Bundt and listening for a heartbeat. I want to laugh but I don't let myself. Olly looks up and shakes his head solemnly. I close my curtains, suppressing a smile, and walk away.

NIGHT SEVEN

I TELL MYSELF that I won't look, but as soon as the first ping sounds I'm at the window. Olly is wearing a black bathrobe with an oversized silver cross around his neck. He's performing last rites of the Bundt.

Finally I cannot help it. I laugh and laugh and laugh. He looks up and grins back. He takes a black marker from his pocket and writes on the window:

SORRY ABOUT THE OTHER NIGHT.
GENERICUSER033@GMAIL.COM

FIRST CONTACT, PART TWO

From: Madeline F. Whittier
To: genericuser033@gmail.com
Subject: Hello
Sent: June 4, 8:03 PM

Hello. I guess we should start with introductions? My name
is Madeline Whittier, but you can tell that from my e-mail
address. What's yours?
- Madeline Whittier
P.S. You don't have anything to apologize for.
P.P.S. What is that Bundt made of?

From: genericuser033
To: Madeline F. Whittier<madeline.whittier@gmail.com>
Subject: RE: Hello
Sent: June 4, 8:07 PM

you are a terrible spy madeline whittier if you haven't
already figured out my name. my sister and i tried to meet

you last week, but your mom wasn't having it. i really don't know what the bundt is made of. rocks?

From: Madeline F. Whittier
To: genericuser033@gmail.com
Subject: RE: RE: Hello
Sent: June 4, 8:11 PM

Hi,
Bundt Cake Recipe

3 cups all-purpose cement mix
1 1/4 cups fine-grain sawdust
1 cup gravel (various sizes for added interest)
1/2 tsp salt
1 cup Elmer's Glue
2 sticks unsalted butter
3 tsp paint thinner
4 large eggs (room temperature)

DIRECTIONS

Preheat oven to 350 degrees.
Grease Bundt pan

For the cake
1. In medium bowl, whisk together cement mix, salt, and gravel.

2. In large bowl, whisk together butter, Elmer's Glue, paint thinner, and eggs. Do not overmix.

3. Gradually whisk in dry ingredients in small batches.

4. Spoon batter into Bundt mold.

5. Bake until a tester inserted in cake refuses to come out. Cool in pan on rack.

For the glaze:

1. Whisk together sawdust and enough water to form a thick yet pourable glaze.

2. Set rack with cake over a piece of wax paper (for easy cleanup).

3. Drizzle cake with glaze and let solidify before serving.

(Serves 0)

- Madeline Whittier
P.S. I'm not a spy!

FIRST CONTACT, PART THREE

Q Wednesday, 8:15 P.M.

Olly: i was going to email you back, but saw you were online. your recipe cracked me up. has there ever been a spy in the whole history of spying that's admitted to being a spy? i think not. i'm olly and it's nice to meet you.

Olly: what's the "f" stand for?

Madeline: Furukawa. My mom is 3rd generation Japanese American. I'm half Japanese.

Olly: what's the other half?

Madeline: African American.

Olly: do you have a nickname madeline furukawa whittier or am i expected to call you madeline furukawa whittier?

Madeline: I don't have a nickname. Everyone calls me Madeline. Sometimes my mom calls me honey or sweetie. Does that count?

Olly: no of course it doesn't count. no one calls you m or maddy or mad or maddy-mad-mad-mad? i'll pick one for you.

Olly: we're gonna be friends

Madeline: Since we're going to be friends, I have questions: Where are you from? Why do you wear a cap all the time? Is your head oddly shaped? Why do you only ever wear black? Related question: Are you aware that clothing comes in other colors? I have suggestions if you need them. What do you do on the roof? What's the tattoo on your right arm?

Olly: i have answers: we're from all over, but mostly the east coast. i shaved my head before we moved here (big mistake). yes. i'm dead sexy in black. yes. none needed, thanks. nothing. barcode

Madeline: What have you got against capital letters and proper punctuation?

Olly: who says that i do

Madeline: I have to go. Sorry!

Friday, 8:34 P.M.

Olly: so how grounded are you?

Madeline: I'm not grounded. Why do you think I'm grounded?

Olly: well something made you log off in a hurry last night. i'm guessing it was your mom. trust me i know all about being grounded. and you never leave the house. i haven't seen you outside once since we got here

Madeline: I'm sorry. I don't know what to say. I'm not grounded, but I can't leave the house.

Olly: very mysterious. are you a ghost? that's what i thought the day we moved in and i saw you at the window. and it would be my luck that the pretty girl next door is not actually alive

Madeline: First I was a spy and now I'm a ghost!

Olly: not a ghost? a fairytale princess then. which one are you? cinderella? will you turn into a pumpkin if you leave the house?

Olly: or rapunzel? your hair's pretty long. just let it down and i'll climb up and rescue you

Madeline: That has always sounded impractical and painful don't you think?

Olly: yes. so not cinderella and not rapunzel. snow white then. your evil stepmom put you under a spell so that you can't leave the house and the world will never know how fair you are

Madeline: That's not how the story goes. Did you know that in the original version it wasn't an evil stepmother, it was an evil mother? Can you believe that? Also, there were no dwarves. Interesting, no?

Olly: definitely no

Madeline: I'm not a princess.

Madeline: And I don't need rescuing.

Olly: that's ok. i'm no prince

Madeline: You think I'm pretty?

Olly: for a fairytale ghost spy princess? definitely

Saturday, 8:01 P.M.

Olly: how come you don't log on until after 8?

Madeline: I'm usually not alone until then.

Olly: someone's with you all day?

Madeline: Can we please not talk about this?

Olly: curiouser and curiouser madeline whittier

Sunday, 8:22 P.M.

Olly: here's a game. fast five favorites. book word color vice person

Olly: come on come on. type faster woman. don't think just type

Madeline: Sheesh. The Little Prince. Uxorious. Aquamarine. I don't have any vices. My mom.

Olly: everyone's got vices

Madeline: Not me. Why? How many do you have?

Olly: enough to choose a favorite one

Madeline: OK, your turn.

Olly: same list?

Madeline: Yes

Olly: lord of the flies, macabre, black, stealing silverware, my sister

Madeline: Ugh. Lord of the Flies? I don't think we can be friends anymore. That book is awful.

Olly: what's so awful about it?

Madeline: Everything!

Olly: you just don't like it because it's true

Madeline: What's true? Left to our own devices we would kill each other?

Olly: yes

Madeline: Do you really believe that?

Olly: yes

Madeline: Well, I don't. I definitely don't.

Madeline: Do you really steal silverware?

Olly: you should see my spoon collection

Monday, 8:07 P.M.

Olly: what'd you do to get so grounded?

Madeline: I'm not grounded and I don't want to talk about this.

Olly: does it involve a guy?

Olly: are you knocked up? do you have a boyfriend?

Madeline: Oh my God, you're insane! I'm not pregnant and I don't have a boyfriend! What kind of girl do you think I am?

Olly: a mysterious one

Madeline: Have you spent all day thinking that I was pregnant?

Madeline: Have you?

Olly: it crossed my mind once or twice or fifteen times

Madeline: Unbelievable.

Olly: don't you want to know if i have a girlfriend?

Madeline: No.

Tuesday, 8:18 P.M.

Madeline: Hi.

Olly: hey

Madeline: I didn't know if you'd log on tonight. Are you OK?

Olly: fine

Madeline: What happened? Why was he so angry?

Olly: i don't know what you're talking about

Madeline: Your dad, Olly. Why was he so angry?

Olly: you've got your secrets. i've got mine

Madeline: OK.

Olly: ok

Wednesday, 3:31 A.M.

Olly: couldn't sleep?

Madeline: No.

Olly: me too. fast five favorites movie. food body-part class

Madeline: That's only four. Besides, it's too late for this. I can't think.

Olly: waiting

Madeline: Pride and Prejudice—the BBC version, toast, hands, architecture.

Olly: jesus. is there a girl on this planet who doesn't love mr. darcy

Madeline: All girls love Mr. Darcy?

Olly: are you kidding? even my sister loves darcy and she doesn't love anybody.

Madeline: She must love somebody. I'm sure she loves you.

Olly: what's so great about darcy?

Madeline: That is not a serious question.

Olly: he's a snob

Madeline: But he overcomes it and eventually

realizes that character matters more than class! He's a man open to learning life's lessons! Also, he's completely gorgeous and noble and dark and brooding and poetic. Did I mention gorgeous? Also, he loves Elizabeth beyond all reason.

Olly: huh

Madeline: Yeah.

Olly: my turn?

Madeline: Proceed.

Olly: Godzilla, toast, eyes, math. wait, is the body part your favorite on yourself or on someone else?

Madeline: I don't know! It's your list.

Olly: o yeah. all right, i'm sticking with eyes

Madeline: What color are your eyes?

Olly: blue

Madeline: Be more specific, please.

Olly: jesus. girls. ocean blue

Madeline: Atlantic or Pacific?

Olly: atlantic. What color are yours?

Madeline: Chocolate brown.

Olly: more specific please

Madeline: 75% cacao butter dark chocolate brown.

Olly: hehe. nice.

Madeline: That was still only four favorites. We need one more.

Olly: i leave it to you

Madeline: Form of poetry.

Olly: that assumes that I have one

Madeline: You're not a heathen.

Olly: limericks

Madeline: You are a heathen. I'm going to pretend you didn't say that.

Olly: what's wrong with a good limerick?

Madeline: "Good limerick" is a contradiction in terms.

Olly: what's your favorite?

Madeline: Haiku.

Olly: haikus are awful. they're just less fun limericks

Madeline: You've been downgraded from heathen to heretic.

Olly: noted

Madeline: OK. I should be asleep.

Olly: ok me too.

Q Thursday, 8:00 P.M.

Madeline: I wouldn't have guessed that math was your favorite class.

Olly: why not?

Madeline: I don't know. You climb buildings and leap over things. Most people are good with their bodies or their minds but not both.

Olly: is that a nice way of saying you think i'm dumb?

Madeline: No! I mean that . . . I don't know what I mean.

Olly: you mean i'm too sexy to be good at it. that's ok. i get that a lot

Madeline: . . .

Olly: it just takes practice like anything else. i was a

52

mathlete two high school

got a probability and stats

Madeline: No!

Olly: yes!

Madeline: So sexy.

Olly: i sense insincerity

Madeline: No!

Olly: yes!

Madeline: :) So are you going to be a Mathlete at SFV High?

Olly: probably not

Olly: my dad made me quit. he wanted me to do something more manly like football

Madeline: You play football?

Olly: no. he made me quit the mathletes, but he couldn't bully the coach into taking me midseason. he let it go eventually

Madeline: What if he brings it up again now?

Olly: i'm a little harder to bully now than i was 2 years ago

Olly: i'm meaner now. bigger too

Madeline: You don't seem mean.

Olly: you don't know me that well yet

Friday, 3:03 A.M.

Madeline: You're awake again.

Olly: yeah

Madeline: I know you don't want to talk about this.

Olly: and yet

w what happened today. Is your mom

e's ok. it's not the first time. it's not the last
e

Madeline: Oh, Olly.

Olly: please don't oh olly me

Olly: tell me something, anything. tell me something funny

Madeline: OK. Why was the boy surprised to find celery growing out of his ears?

Olly: why?

Madeline: Because he'd planted corn!

Madeline: Hello?

Olly: oh jesus. that is not a good joke

Madeline: Made you smile though.

Olly: yeah it did

Olly: thanks

Madeline: Anytime.

Q Saturday, 8:01 P.M.

Olly: i guess i won't get to meet you in person until school starts

Madeline: I don't go to school.

Olly: you mean you don't go to SF Valley High? where do you go?

Madeline: I mean I don't go to regular school. I go online.

Olly: why?

54

Madeline: I really can't talk about this.

Olly: come on. you gotta give me something here

Madeline: I want us to be friends. I don't want you to feel sorry for me.

Olly: just tell me. we're still gonna be friends

Madeline: I'm sick.

Olly: how sick?

Madeline: Really sick. Can't leave the house sick.

Olly: jesus

Olly: are you dying?

Madeline: Not right now, no.

Olly: soon?

Madeline: If I left the house, yes.

Olly: ok

Olly: we're still friends. i don't feel sorry for you

Madeline: Thank you.

Olly: how does the school thing work?

Madeline: All my classes are over Skype. I have homework and quizzes and grades. Lots of people are homeschooled.

Olly: huh. cool

Olly: ever notice how a lot of the national spelling bee finalists are all homeschooled?

Madeline: I've never noticed that.

Olly: it's a thing

Olly: i wish we could meet

Madeline: Me too.

Madeline: OK, I need to go now.

Olly: go then

Olly: you still there?

Madeline: Yes.

Olly: come to the window

Madeline: Now? I'm wearing my nightgown.

Olly: put on a robe. come to the window so that I can see you

Madeline: OK, I'll be right there. Good night, Olly.

Olly: goodnight maddy

ASTRONAUT ICE CREAM

"MR. WATERMAN'S ON his way up," Carla says from the doorway. I'm finally putting the finishing touches on my model for architecture class. I've had to cut short two nights of IMs with Olly to get it done. I don't want my mom to get worried again. The assignment was to design an outdoor shopping/dining center in my favorite style. I chose art deco because the buildings look like they're flying even though they're standing still.

The centerpiece of the complex is a grassy outdoor seating area populated with oversized, oddly shaped chairs painted in bright zigzag patterns. I've already "planted" miniature plastic palm trees in the grass, and now I'm strategically placing miniature plastic people holding miniature plastic shopping bags to give it the "vigor of life," as Mr. Waterman would say.

In two years of tutoring I've only met Mr. Waterman in person twice. Usually all of my tutoring, including architecture, takes place via Skype. My mom made a special exception this week. I think she's still feeling bad about Kara and Olly's visit from a couple of weeks ago. I told her she had nothing to feel bad about, but she insisted. Having a visitor is a big deal because they have to agree to a medical background check and a thorough physical. Also they have to be decontaminated, which is basically like getting a high-speed air bath for about an hour. It's a pain to come see me.

Mr. Waterman bustles in looking merry but harried, like Santa Claus on Christmas Eve just before the big ride. The decontamination process makes him cold, so he's rubbing his hands together and blowing on them for warmth.

"Madeline," he says happily, clapping his hands together. He's my favorite of all my tutors. He never looks at me pityingly and he loves architecture like I love architecture. If I were going to be something when I grew up, an architect is what I would be.

"Hi, Mr. Waterman." I smile awkwardly, not really knowing how to be around someone who's not Carla or my mother.

"So what have we got here?" he asks, gray eyes twinkling. I place my last two tiny shoppers next to a toy store and stand back.

He circles the model sometimes beaming, sometimes frowning, all the while making weird clucking sounds.

"Well, dear, you've outdone yourself. This is quite lovely!" He straightens from the model and is about to pat me on the shoulder before he catches himself. No touching allowed. He shakes his head slightly and then bends over to examine some more.

"Yes, yes, quite lovely. There are only a few things we should talk about. But, first! Where is our astronaut hiding?"

Whenever I make a new model I make a clay astronaut figure and hide him in it. Each figure is different. This time he's in full astronaut gear complete with airtight helmet and bulky oxygen tank, sitting in the diner at a table piled high with food. I've made miniature banana split sundaes, blueberry pancake stacks, scrambled eggs, toast with butter and marmalade, bacon, milk shakes (strawberry, chocolate, and vanilla), cheeseburgers, and fries. I'd wanted to make curly fries but I ran out of time and had to settle for just regular fries.

"There he is!" Mr. Waterman exclaims. He clucks at the scene for a few moments and then turns to me. His merry eyes are a little less merry than usual. "It's just wonderful, my dear. But how will he eat all that scrumptious food with his helmet on?"

I look back at my astronaut. It'd never occurred to me that he'd want to eat the food.

EVERYTHING'S A RISK

CARLA'S SMILING AT me like she knows something I don't know. She's been doing it all day whenever she thinks I'm not looking. Also she's been singing "Take a Chance on Me" by ABBA, her absolute favorite band of all time. She's breathtakingly out of tune. I'll have to ask Olly the probability that she could miss every single note. Shouldn't she hit one just by random chance?

It's 12:30 P.M. and I have a half hour for lunch before my history tutor comes online. I'm not hungry. I'm basically never hungry anymore. Apparently a body can exist on IM alone.

Carla's not looking, so I tab over to my Gmail. Thirteen messages from Olly since last night. They're all sent around 3 A.M. and, naturally, he doesn't write a subject. I laugh a little and shake my head.

I want to read them, am dying to read them, but I have to be careful with Carla in the room. I glance over and find her staring back at me, eyebrows raised. Does she know something?

"What's so interesting on that laptop?" she asks. God. She definitely knows.

I draw my chair closer to the desk and place my sandwich on the laptop.

"Nothing." I take a bite of the sandwich. It's Turkey Tuesday.

"It's not nothing. Something is making you laugh over there." She inches closer, smiling at me. Her brown eyes crinkle at the corners and her smile reaches the edge of her face.

"Cat video," I say through a mouthful of turkey. Ugh, wrong thing to say. Carla lives for cat videos. She thinks they're the only thing the Internet is good for.

She comes around, stands behind me, and reaches for the laptop.

I drop my sandwich and hug the laptop close to my chest. I'm not a good liar, and I say the first thing that pops into my head. "You don't want to see this one, Carla. It's bad. The cat dies."

We stare at each other in a kind of shocked standoff for a few seconds. I'm shocked because I'm an idiot and I can't believe that I said that. Carla's shocked because I'm an idiot and she can't believe that I said that. Her mouth drops open comically, like a cartoon, and her big round eyes get even bigger and rounder. She bends over at the waist, slaps her knee, and laughs like I've never heard her laugh. Who actually slaps their knee while laughing?

"You mean to tell me the only thing you could think to say was that it was a dead cat?" She's laughing again.

"So you know."

"Well, if I didn't know before I would surely know now."

She laughs a little more, slaps her knee again. "Oh, you should've seen your face."

"It's not *that* funny," I grumble, annoyed that I gave myself away.

"You forget I have one of you at home. I always know when

Rosa is up to no good. Besides, you, Miss Thing, are not any good at hiding things. I see you checking your e-mail and looking for him out the window."

I put my laptop back down on the desk. "So, you're not mad at me?" I ask, relieved.

She hands me my sandwich. "It depends. Why were you hiding it from me?"

"I didn't want you to worry about me getting sad again."

She eyes me for a long second. "Do I need to worry?"

"No."

"Then I'm not worrying." She brushes my hair back from my shoulders. "Eat," she says.

FIFTEEN MINUTES LATER

"MAYBE HE COULD come over for a visit?"

I've surprised myself by asking, but Carla's not surprised at all. She doesn't even pause from wiping away nonexistent dust from my bookshelf.

"Teenagers are the same all over. Give them an inch and they'll take a mile."

"Is that a no?" I ask.

She laughs at me.

TWO HOURS LATER

I TRY AGAIN. "It would only be for half an hour. He could get decontaminated like Mr. Waterman and then—"

"Are you crazy?"

TEN MINUTES AFTER THAT

"FIFTEEN MINUTES?"

"No."

LATER STILL

"PLEASE, CARLA—"

She cuts me off. "And here I thought you were doing fine."

"I am. I am doing fine. I just want to meet him—"

"We can't always get what we want," she says. From the flatness of her tone alone, I know it's a phrase she uses on Rosa all the time. I can tell she regrets saying it to me, but still she doesn't say anything else.

She's leaving for the day, halfway out my bedroom door when she stops. "You know I don't like saying no to you. You're a good girl."

I rush right through this opening. "He'd get decontaminated and sit across the room, far, far away from me and only for fifteen minutes. Thirty minutes at the most."

She shakes her head, but it's not a firm shake. "It's too risky. And your mother would never allow it."

"We won't tell her," I say instantly.

She gives me a sharp, disappointed look. "Do you girls really find it so easy to lie to your mamas?"

TO THOSE WHO WAIT

CARLA DOESN'T SAY anything about it again until just after lunch two days later.

"Now. You listen to me," she says. "No touching. You stay on your side of the room and he stays on his. I already told him the same thing."

I understand the words she's saying, but I don't understand *what* she's saying.

"What do you mean? You mean he's here? He's already here?"

"You stay on your side and he stays on his. No touching. You understand?"

I don't, but I nod yes anyway.

"He's waiting for you in the sunroom."

"Decontaminated?"

The look on her face says *what do you take me for?*

I stand up, sit down, and stand up again.

"Oh, Lordy," she says. "Go fix yourself up fast. I'm only giving you twenty minutes."

My stomach doesn't just flip, it does high-wire somersaults without a net. "What made you change your mind?"

She comes over, takes my chin in her hand, and stares into my eyes for such a long time that I start to fidget. I can see her sorting through all she wants to say.

In the end all she says is: "You deserve a little something."

This is how Rosa gets everything she wants. She simply asks for it from her mother with the too-big heart.

I head to the mirror to "fix myself." I've almost forgotten what I look like. I don't spend a lot of time looking. There's no need when there's no one to see you. I like to think that I'm an exact fifty-fifty mixture of my mom and dad. My warm brown skin is what you get by mixing her pale olive skin with his richer dark brown. My hair is big and long and wavy, not as curly as his, but not as straight as hers. Even my eyes are a perfect blend—neither Asian nor African but somewhere in between.

I look away and then look back quickly, trying to catch myself unawares to get a more accurate picture, trying to see what Olly will see. I try out a laugh and then smile, with teeth and without. I even try out a frown, though I'm hoping I won't have cause to use it.

Carla watches my antics in the mirror, amused and bemused at the same time.

"I almost remember when I was your age," she says.

I don't turn around, talking instead to the Carla in the mirror. "Are you sure about this? You don't think it's too risky anymore?"

"You trying to talk me out of it?" She comes over and puts a hand on my shoulder. "Everything's a risk. Not doing anything is a risk. It's up to you."

I look around my white room at my white couch and shelves, my white walls, all of it safe and familiar and unchanging.

I think of Olly, decontamination-cold and waiting for me. He's the opposite of all these things. He's not safe. He's not familiar. He's in constant motion.

He's the biggest risk I've ever taken.

FUTURE PERFECT

From: Madeline F. Whittier

To: genericuser033@gmail.com

Subject: Future Perfect

Sent: July 10, 12:30 PM

By the time you read this we will have met. It will have been perfect.

OLLY

THE SUNROOM IS my favorite room in the house. It's almost all glass—glass roof and floor-to-ceiling glass windows that look out onto our perfectly manicured back lawn.

The room's decor is like a movie set of a tropical rain forest. It's filled with realistic and lush-looking fake tropical plants. Banana and coconut trees laden with fake fruit and hibiscus plants with fake flowers are everywhere. There's even a babbling stream that snakes its way through the room, but there are no fish—at least no real ones. The furniture is aged white wicker that looks like it's been sitting in the sun. Because it's meant to be tropical, my mom keeps a heated fan running and a slightly too-warm breeze fills the room.

Most days I love it because I can imagine that the glass has fallen away and I'm Outside. Other days I feel like a fish in an aquarium.

By the time I get there, Olly has managed to climb halfway up the rocky back wall, hands and feet wedged into crevices. He's pinching one of the large banana leaves between his fingers when I walk in.

"It's not real," he says to me.

"It's not real," I say at the same time.

He lets go of the branch but remains where he is on the wall. Climbing for him is like walking for the rest of us.

"Are you going to stay up there?" I ask, because I don't know what else to say.

"I'm thinking about it, Maddy. Carla said I had to stay as far away from you as possible and she doesn't seem like the kind of lady that you piss off."

"You can come down," I say. "Carla's not as scary as she seems."

"OK." He slips effortlessly to the floor. He puts his hands into his pockets, crosses his feet at the ankles, and leans back against the wall. I don't think I've ever seen him so still. I think he's trying not to spook me.

"Maybe you should come in," he says, and then I realize that I'm still in the doorway holding on to the knob. I close the door but don't take my eyes off him. His eyes track my movements as well.

After all the IMs I felt like I knew him, but now with him standing in front of me it doesn't feel that way at all. He's taller than I thought and way more muscled, but not bulky. His arms are lean and sculpted and his biceps fill the sleeves of his black T-shirt. His skin is a tanned golden brown. It would be warm to touch.

"You're different than I thought you'd be," I blurt out.

He grins and a dimple forms just under his right eye.

"I know. Sexier, right? It's OK, you can say it."

I guffaw. "How do you manage to carry around an ego that size and weight?"

"It's the muscles," he shoots back, flexing his biceps and raising a single comical eyebrow.

Some of my nervousness falls away but then comes right back when he watches me laugh without saying anything for a few seconds too long.

"Your hair really is so long," he says. "And you never said you had freckles."

"Was I supposed to?"

"Freckles might be a deal breaker." He smiles and the dimple comes back. Cute.

I move to the couch and sit. He leans against the rock wall across the room.

"They're the bane of my existence," I say, referring to the freckles. This is a ridiculous thing to say because, of course, the bane of my existence is that I'm sick and unable to leave my house. We both realize this at the same time and then we're both laughing again.

"You're funny," he says after our laughter subsides.

I smile. I've never thought of myself as a funny girl, but I'm happy that he thinks so.

We are awkward together for a few moments, unsure what to say. The silence would be much less noticeable over IM. We could chalk it up to any number of distractions. But right now, in real life, it feels like we both have blank thought balloons over our heads. Actually, mine's not blank at all, but I really can't tell him how beautiful his eyes are. They're Atlantic Ocean blue, just like he'd said. It's strange because of course I'd known that. But the difference between knowing it and seeing them in person is the difference between dreaming of flying and flight.

"This is some crazy room," he says, looking around.

"Yeah. My mom built it so I could feel like I was outside."

"Does it work?"

"Most days. I have a really excellent imagination."

"You really are a fairy tale. *Princess Madeline and the Glass Castle.*" He's quiet again, like he's trying to build up to something.

"It's OK to ask me," I say.

He's wearing a single black rubber band around his wrist and he pulls at it a few times before continuing. "How long have you been sick?"

"My whole life."

"What would happen if you went outside?"

"My head would explode. Or my lungs. Or my heart."

"How can you joke . . . ?"

I shrug. "How can I not? Besides, I try not to want things I can't have."

"You're like a Zen master. You should teach a class."

"It takes a long time to learn." I smile back at him.

He crouches and then sits, back against the wall, forearms on his knees. Even though he's still, I can feel the need to move coming off of him. The boy is kinetic energy.

"Where do you want to go the most?" he asks.

"Besides outer space?"

"Yes, Maddy, besides outer space." I like the way he says Maddy, as if he's been calling me that my whole life.

"The beach. The ocean."

"Want me to describe it for you?"

I nod more vigorously than I expected to. My heart speeds up like I'm doing something illicit.

"I've seen pictures and videos, but what's it like to actually be in the water? Is it like taking a bath in a giant tub?"

"Sort of," he says slowly, considering. "No, I take it back. Taking a bath is relaxing. Being in the ocean is scary. It's wet and cold and salty and deadly."

That's not what I was expecting. "You hate the ocean?"

He's grinning now, warming to his topic. "I don't hate it. I respect it." He holds up a single finger. "Respect. It's Mother Nature at her finest—awesome, beautiful, impersonal, murderous. Think about it. All that water and you could still die of thirst. And the whole point of waves is to suck your feet from under you so that you drown faster. The ocean will swallow you whole and burp you out and not notice you were even there."

"Oh my God, you're scared of it!"

"We haven't even gotten to great white sharks or saltwater crocodiles or Indonesian needlefish or—"

"OK, OK," I say, laughing and holding up my hands for him to stop.

"It's no joke," he says with mock seriousness. "The ocean will kill you." He winks at me. "It turns out that Mother Nature is a lousy mom."

I'm too busy laughing to say anything.

"So, what else do you want to know?"

"After that? Nothing!"

"Come on. I'm a fount of knowledge."

"OK, do one of your crazy tricks for me."

He's on his feet in a blink and begins assessing the room critically. "There's not enough room. Let's go out—" He stops himself midsentence. "Crap, Maddy, I'm sorry."

"Stop," I say. I stand up and hold a hand out. "Do not feel sorry for me." I say this harshly, but it's too important a point. I couldn't stand pity coming from him.

He flicks his rubber band, nods once, and lets it go. "I can do a one-armed handstand."

He steps away from the wall and simply falls forward until he's upside down on his hands. It's such a graceful and effortless movement that I'm momentarily filled with envy. What's it like to have such complete confidence in your body and what it will do?

"That's amazing," I whisper.

"We're not in church," he whisper-shouts back, voice slightly strained from being upside down.

"I don't know," I say. "It feels like I should be quiet."

He doesn't answer. Instead, he closes his eyes, slowly removes his left hand from the floor, and holds it out to the side. He's almost perfectly still. The quiet bubbling of the pond and his slightly heavier breathing are the only sounds in the room. His T-shirt falls up and I can see the hard muscles of his stomach. The skin is the same warm, golden tan. I pull my eyes away.

"OK," I say, "you can stop now."

He's upright again before I can blink.

"What else can you do?"

He rubs his hands together and grins back at me.

One backflip later he sits back down against the wall and closes his eyes.

"So, why outer space first?" he asks.

I shrug. "I want to see the world, I guess."

"Not what most people mean by that," he says, smiling.

I nod and close my eyes as well. "Do you ever feel—" I begin, but then the door opens and Carla bustles in to rush him out.

"You didn't touch, right?" she asks, arms akimbo.

We both open our eyes and stare at each other. All at once I'm hyperaware of his body and mine.

"There was no touching," Olly confirms, his eyes never leaving my face. Something in his tone makes me blush hard, and heat travels a slow wave across my face and chest.

Spontaneous combustion is a real thing. I'm certain of it.

DIAGNOSIS

webdoc.com

HYSTERICAL ABDOMINAL RHOPALOCERA

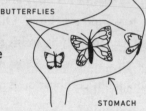

BUTTERFLIES

STOMACH

The condition of having one or more monarch butterflies take up residence in the stomach.

WHO IS AFFECTED BY HAR?
The disease affects at least one teenaged American girl every 30 seconds.

SYMPTOMS
- Nausea
- Elevated heart rate
- Inability to focus
- Stomach "flipping"
- Light-headedness

CAUSES
HAR episodes are usually triggered by contact with a romantic interest. HAR sufferers describe feeling symptoms not only during the contact but before and after as well. Patients with the most acute form of the disease can trigger an episode by simply thinking about their romantic interest. Coupled with an inability to stop thinking about said interest, the disease [read more]

PERSPECTIVES

BEFORE CARLA ARRIVES the next morning I spend exactly thirteen minutes in bed convinced that I am getting sick. It takes her exactly six minutes to un-convince me. She takes my temperature, blood pressure, heart and pulse rates before declaring that I am simply lovesick.

"Classic symptoms," she says.

"I'm not in love. I can't be in love."

"And why not?"

"What would be the point?" I say, throwing my hands up. "Me in love would be like being a food critic with no taste buds. It would be like being a color-blind painter. It would be like—"

"Like skinny-dipping by yourself."

I have to laugh at that one. "Exactly," I say. "Pointless."

"Not pointless," she says, and looks at me seriously. "Just because you can't experience everything doesn't mean you shouldn't experience anything. Besides, doomed love is a part of life."

"I'm not in love," I say again.

"And you're not sick," she retorts. "So there's nothing to worry about."

*

For the rest of the morning I'm too distracted to read or do homework. Despite Carla's reassurances that I'm not getting sick, I find myself paying too close attention to my body and how it feels. Are my fingertips tingling? Do they usually do that? Why can't I seem to catch my breath? How many somersaults can a stomach do before becoming irreparably knotted? I ask Carla to do an extra check of my vitals, and the results are all normal.

By the afternoon I acknowledge in my head that Carla might be onto something. I might not be in *love*, but I'm in *like*. I'm in serious *like*. I wander the house aimlessly, seeing Olly everywhere. I see him in my kitchen making stacks of toast for dinner. I see him in my living room suffering though *Pride and Prejudice* with me. I see him in my bedroom, his black-clad body asleep on my white couch.

And it's not just Olly that I see. I keep picturing myself floating high above the earth. From the edge of space I can see the whole world all at once. My eyes don't have to stop at a wall or at a door. I can see the beginning and the end of time. I can see infinity from there.

For the first time in a long time, I want more than I have.

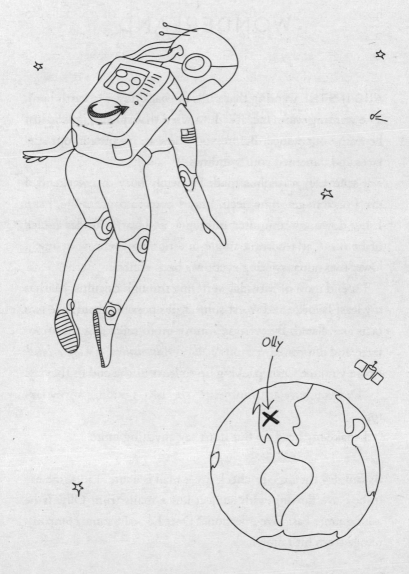

Olly

WONDERLAND

AND IT'S THE wanting that pulls me back down to earth hard. The wanting scares me. It's like a weed that spreads slowly, just beneath your notice. Before you know it, it's pitted your surfaces and darkened your windows.

I send Olly a single e-mail. I'm really busy this weekend, I say. I need to get some sleep, I say. I need to concentrate, I say. I shut down my computer, unplug it, and bury it under a stack of books. Carla raises a single questioning eyebrow at me. I lower two nonanswering eyebrows back at her.

I spend most of Saturday suffering through calculus. Math is my least favorite and worst subject. It's possible that those two facts are related. By evening I move on to rereading the annotated and illustrated version of *Alice's Adventures in Wonderland*. I barely notice Carla packing up to leave at the end of the day.

"Did you have an argument?" she asks, nodding at my laptop.

I shake my head no but don't say anything more.

By Sunday the urge to check my e-mail is acute. I imagine my in-box overflowing with subject-less e-mails from Olly. Is he asking more Fast Five questions? Does he want some company, refuge from his family?

"You're OK," Carla says on her way out the door that evening. She kisses my forehead, and I'm a little girl again.

I take *Alice* to my white couch and settle in. Carla's right of course. I am OK, but, like Alice, I'm just trying not to get lost. I keeping thinking about the summer I turned eight. I spent so many days with my forehead pressed against my glass window, bruising myself with my futile wanting. At first I just wanted to look out the window. But then I wanted to go outside. And then I wanted to play with the neighborhood kids, to play with all kids everywhere, to be normal for just an afternoon, a day, a lifetime.

So. I don't check my e-mail. One thing I'm certain of: Wanting just leads to more wanting. There's no end to desire.

LIFE IS SHORT™
SPOILER REVIEWS BY MADELINE

ALICE'S ADVENTURES IN WONDERLAND BY LEWIS CARROLL
Spoiler alert: Beware the Queen of Hearts. She'll have your head.

MAKES YOU STRONGER

THERE'S NO E-MAIL from Olly. Not one. I even check my spam folder. This shouldn't bother me and it doesn't. It doesn't bother me a lot. In the interest of thoroughness, I refresh my e-mail three more times in about two seconds. Maybe it's just hiding somewhere, stuck behind another one.

Carla walks in as I'm about to refresh again.

"I didn't think you'd be able to unearth that thing," she says.

"Good morning to you, too," I say, squinting down at the screen.

She smiles and begins her daily unpacking-of-the-medical-bag ritual. Why she doesn't leave it here overnight is a mystery.

"Why are you frowning? Another dead cat video?" Her smile is toothy and wide, very Cheshire Cat–like. Any minute now her body will disappear, leaving just a grinning floating head in its wake.

"Olly didn't send me any e-mails."

I believe *nonplussed* is the word for her expression.

"All weekend," I say, by way of illumination.

"I see." She puts the stethoscope in her ears and the thermometer under my tongue.

"Did you e-mail him?"

"Yesh." I talk around the thermometer.

"Don't talk, just nod."

"Sawwy."

She rolls her eyes and we wait for the beep.

"Ninety-nine point eight," I say, handing the thermometer back to her. "I basically told him not to write. Am I being ridiculous?"

She motions for me to turn around so she can listen to my lungs but doesn't respond.

"How ridiculous?" I prompt. "On a scale of one to ten, one being perfectly rational and reasonable and ten being absurd and certifiable."

"About an eight," she says without hesitation.

I'd been expecting her to say twelve, so eight seems like a victory. I tell her so and she laughs at me.

"So you told him not to write to you and then he didn't write to you. This is what you're telling me?"

"Well, I didn't say DON'T WRITE in big, bold letters or anything. I just said I was busy." I think she's going to make fun of me, but she doesn't.

"Why didn't you write to him?"

"Because of what we talked about. I like him, Carla. A lot. Too much."

The look on her face says *is that all?* "Do you really want to lose the only friend you've ever had over a little bit of heartache?"

I've read many, many books involving heartache. Not one has ever described it as little. Soul-shattering and world-destroying, yes. Little, no.

She leans back against the couch. "You don't know this yet, but this will pass. It's just the newness and hormones."

Maybe she's right. I want her to be right so I can talk to him again.

She leans forward and winks at me. "That, and he's cute."

"He *is* pretty cute, right?" I giggle.

"Honey, I didn't think they made them like that anymore!"

I'm laughing, too, and imagining a factory with little Ollys coming off an assembly line. How would they ever keep them still enough to package and mail?

"Go!" She slaps my knee. "You have enough things to be afraid of. Love can't kill you."

NO YES MAYBE

Monday, 8:09 P.M.

Madeline: Hi.

Olly: hey

Madeline: How are you? How was your weekend?

Olly: fine. good

Olly: yours?

Madeline: Good, but busy. I mostly did calculus homework.

Olly: ahh, calculus. the mathematics of change

Madeline: Wow. You really weren't kidding about liking math?

Olly: no

Madeline: I'm sorry about my e-mail.

Olly: which part?

Madeline: All of it. Are you upset with me? No, yes, maybe?

Olly: no yes maybe

Madeline: I don't think you're supposed to use all the answers.

Olly: why'd you send it?

Madeline: I got scared.

Olly: of what?

Madeline: You.

Madeline: You didn't write to me either.

Olly: you didn't want me to

Madeline: . . .

Olly: does the ellipsis mean we're having an awkward silence or that you're thinking?

Madeline: Both.

Madeline: Why do you like math so much?

Olly: why do you like books so much?

Madeline: Those are not the same thing!

Olly: why not?

Madeline: You can find the meaning of life in a book.

Olly: life has meaning?

Madeline: You're not serious.

Olly: it's possible

Olly: what book can you find the meaning of life in?

Madeline: OK, maybe not just a single book, but if you read enough you'll get there.

Olly: is that your plan?

Madeline: Well, I've got the time.

Madeline: . . .

Olly: thinking?

Madeline: Yes. I have a solution to our problem.

Olly: listening

Madeline: Let's agree to just be friends, ok?

Olly: ok

Olly: but no more checking out my muscles

Madeline: Friends, Olly!

Olly: and my eyes

Madeline: No more talking about my freckles.

Madeline: And my hair.

Olly: and your lips

Madeline: And your dimple.

Olly: you like my dimple?

Madeline: Friends!

Olly: ok

TIME

CARLA MAKES US wait a week before we can see each other again. She wants to be absolutely sure that being in the same room with Olly didn't activate any of my triggers. Even though I agree with her that we should wait just to be safe, the week seems interminable. I'm sort of convinced that time has literally, and not just metaphorically, slowed down, but that's the kind of thing that would make headlines.

EXERCISE A
measure shadows

12pm   4pm

1 cm   7 cm
wow!!

EXERCISE B
watch glue dry

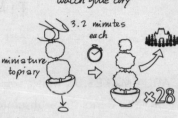

3.2 minutes each

miniature topiary

×28

EXERCISE C
refresh emails

INBOX (0) ⇨ INBOX ⇦ INBOX (0)

EXERCISE D
rearrange books

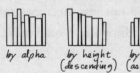

by alpha   by height (descending)   by height (ascending)

CHART: PERCEIVED VS. ACTUAL TIME

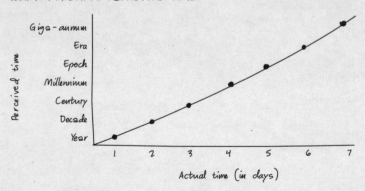

Perceived time

Giga-annum
Era
Epoch
Millennium
Century
Decade
Year

1   2   3   4   5   6   7

Actual time (in days)

SIGNATURE _____

READ + UNDERSTOOD _____

MIRROR, MIRROR

AFTER AN EPOCH, the week finally ends. I'm giddy and trying not to be. This is more difficult than you'd imagine. Trying not to smile only makes you smile more.

Carla watches me struggle to choose what to wear. It's not something I've ever given much thought to. Really, I've never given any thought to it. My closet consists entirely of white T-shirts and blue jeans. The jeans are arranged by type—straight, skinny, boot cut, wide leg, the ridiculously named "boyfriend." My shoes—all Keds, all white—are piled in a heap in the back corner. I almost never wear shoes around the house and now I'm not sure that I can find a pair that will fit. Rummaging through the pile, I find a left and right one of the same size. They fit, but just barely. I stand in front of the mirror. Is your shirt supposed to match your shoes or is that your purse? Is white the best color for my chestnut complexion? I make a mental note to do some shopping later. I'll buy a T-shirt in every color until I find the one that suits me best.

For the fifth time I ask Carla if my mom has already left.

"You know your mother," she says. "Has she ever been late a day in her life?"

My mother believes in punctuality the way other people believe in God. Time is precious, she says, and it's rude to waste someone else's. I'm not even allowed to be late for Friday Night Dinners.

I look at myself in the mirror, change the V-necked white T-shirt for a scoop-neck white T-shirt for no reason at all. Or not for no reason. But to have something to do while waiting for Olly.

I wish again that I could talk to my mom about this. I want to ask her why I get breathless when I think of him. I want to share my giddiness with her. I want to tell her all the funny things Olly says. I want to tell her how I can't make myself stop thinking about him even though I try. I want to ask her if this is the way she felt about Dad at the beginning.

I tell myself it's OK. I didn't get sick after the last time I saw him, and he knows the rules—no touching, full decontamination treatment, no visit if he even suspects he could get sick in the next few days.

I tell myself there's no harm in lying to my mom. I tell myself I won't get sick. I tell myself there's no harm in friendship.

That Carla is right, and love can't kill me.

FORECAST

OLLY'S ON THE wall again when I enter the room. This time he's climbed all the way to the top.

"Don't your fingertips ever get tired?" I ask.

"I've got them on a strict workout regimen," he says, grinning at me. My stomach does a little flip thing that I'm really going to have to get used to, since it seems to be a side effect of seeing him.

I was in this room to do my homework yesterday. I know it's exactly the same as I left it, but it looks and feels different. The room is so much more alive with Olly in it. If all the fake plants and trees swayed to life right now, I wouldn't be surprised.

I walk to the couch and settle into the corner farthest away from him.

Down from the wall, he sits cross-legged and leans his back against it.

I tuck my legs beneath me, adjust my mass of hair, hug my waist. What is it about being in the same room with him that makes me so conscious of my body and all its parts? He even makes me aware of my skin.

"You're wearing shoes today," he says, notices. He's definitely a noticer, the kind of boy who would know if you'd rearranged a painting or added a new vase to a room.

I look down at my shoes. "I have nine pairs of these exact same shoes."

"And you complain about my wardrobe choices?"

"You only wear black! It makes you look sepulchral."

"I need a dictionary to talk to you."

"Of or relating to a sepulcher."

"Not that helpful a definition."

"Basically you're the angel of death."

He grins at me. "The scythe gave me away, didn't it? I thought I hid it so well."

He changes positions. Now he's lying flat on his back, knees bent, hands laced behind his head.

I shift my body again for no reason, pulling my legs into my chest and wrapping my arms around them. Our bodies are having their own conversation separate and apart from us. Is this the difference between friendship and something else? This awareness that I have of him?

The air filters cycle on, making a low hum beneath the sound of the fan.

"How does that work?" His eyes are scanning the ceiling.

"It's industrial. The windows are sealed so air only comes in through the filters on the roof. Nothing over 0.3 microns gets in. Also, the circulation system completely changes all the air in the house every four hours."

"Wow." He turns his head to look at me and I can see him trying to come to terms with just how sick I am.

I look away. "The settlement paid for it." Before he can ask

I add: "The trucker who killed my dad and brother fell asleep behind the wheel. He'd been working three shifts in a row. They settled with my mom."

He turns his head back toward the ceiling. "I'm sorry."

"It's strange because I don't really remember them. Meaning I don't remember them at all." I try to ignore the feelings that surface when I think about them. There's sadness that's not quite sadness, and then guilt. "It's weird to miss something you've never had—or don't remember having, anyway."

"Not so weird," he says. We're both quiet and he closes his eyes.

"Do you ever wonder what your life would be like if you could just change one thing?" he asks.

Not usually, but I'm starting to. What if I weren't sick? What if my dad and brother hadn't died? Not wondering about impossible things is how I've managed to be relatively Zen.

"Everyone thinks they're special," he says. "Everyone's a snowflake, right? We're all unique and complicated. We can never know the human heart, and all that?"

I nod slowly, certain I agree with what he's saying now, but equally certain that I'm going to disagree with whatever's next.

"I think that's nonsense. We're not snowflakes. We're just outputs for a set of inputs."

I stop nodding. "Like a formula?"

"Exactly like a formula." He props himself up to his elbows and looks at me. "I think there are one or two inputs that matter the most. Figure those out and you've figured out the person. You can predict anything about them."

"Really? What am I going to say now?"

He winks at me. "You think I'm a brute, a heretic, a—"

"A crackpot," I complete for him. "You don't really believe we're math equations?"

"I might." He lies back down.

"But how do you know which input to change?" I ask.

He sighs a long, suffering sigh. "Yeah, that's the problem. Even if you could figure out which one to change, then how much should you change it? And what if you can't change it precisely enough? Then you couldn't predict the new output. You could make things worse."

He sits up again. "Imagine, though, if you could just change the right inputs; you could fix things before they went wrong." He says this last part quietly, but with the frustration of someone who's been trying to solve the same unsolvable problem for a long time now. Our eyes meet and he looks embarrassed, like he's revealed more than he meant to.

He lies back down and throws a forearm across his eyes. "The problem is chaos theory. There are too many inputs to the formula and even the small ones matter more than you think. And you can never measure them precisely enough. But! If you could, you could write a formula to predict the weather, the future, people."

"But chaos theory says you can't?"

"Yup."

"You needed a whole branch of mathematics to tell you that people are unpredictable?"

"Had that figured out, did you?"

"Books, Olly! I learned it from books!"

He laughs, rolls onto his side, and laughs some more. He's infectious and I'm laughing, too, my whole body responding to him. I watch for the dimple that I'm no longer supposed to be paying attention to. I want to put my finger into it and keep him smiling forever.

Maybe we can't predict everything, but we can predict some things. For example, I am certainly going to fall in love with Olly.

It's almost certainly going to be a disaster.

MADELINE'S DICTIONARY

ob•ses•sion (əbˈseSHən) *n. pl.* **-s.**
1. acute (and completely justifiable)
interest in something (or someone)
acutely interesting. [2015, *Whittier*]

SECRETS

MY CONSTANT IMING with Olly is catching up with me. I fall asleep during not one but two movie nights with my mom. She begins worrying that something's wrong, that my immune system is compromised somehow. I tell her it's simpler than that. I'm just not getting enough sleep. I guess I understand why, given our situation, her doctor's brain would go immediately to the worst-case scenario. She tells me what I already know, that lack of sleep is not good for someone with my condition. I promise to be better. That night I only IM with him until 2 A.M. instead of our usual 3 A.M.

It feels strange not to talk to my mom about something, some*one*, who's becoming so important to me. My mom and I are drifting apart, but not because we're spending less time together. And not because Olly's replacing her. We're drifting apart because for the first time in my life, I have a secret to keep.

THANK YOU FOR SHOPPING

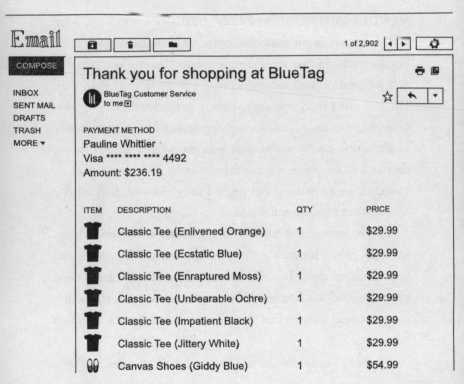

Email

COMPOSE

INBOX
SENT MAIL
DRAFTS
TRASH
MORE ▼

Thank you for shopping at BlueTag

bt BlueTag Customer Service
to me ▼

☆

PAYMENT METHOD
Pauline Whittier
Visa **** **** **** 4492
Amount: $236.19

ITEM	DESCRIPTION	QTY	PRICE
👕	Classic Tee (Enlivened Orange)	1	$29.99
👕	Classic Tee (Ecstatic Blue)	1	$29.99
👕	Classic Tee (Enraptured Moss)	1	$29.99
👕	Classic Tee (Unbearable Ochre)	1	$29.99
👕	Classic Tee (Impatient Black)	1	$29.99
👕	Classic Tee (Jittery White)	1	$29.99
👟	Canvas Shoes (Giddy Blue)	1	$54.99

NUMEROLOGY

NUMBER OF:
minutes it took Olly's dad to begin yelling
after he arrived home last night:
8

complaints about the goddamn roast beef
being overcooked again:
4

times Olly's mom apologized:
6

times Olly's dad called Kara a goddamn freak
for wearing black nail polish:
2

minutes it takes Olly's mom to remove Kara's nail polish:
3

times Olly's dad mentioned that he knows someone
has been drinking his goddamn whiskey:
5

that he's the smartest guy in the house:
2

that no one should forget that he makes all the money:
2

pun-filled jokes it takes to get Olly feeling marginally better
when he IMs at 3 AM:
5

times he writes "it doesn't matter" during our
IM conversation:
7

hours of sleep I got last night:
0

cigarettes Kara buried in the garden this morning:
4

visible bruises on Olly's mom:
0

invisible bruises:
Uncertain

hours until I see Olly again:
0.5

OLLY SAYS

HE'S NOT ON the wall when I see him again the next day. Instead he's in what I've begun to think of as his resting position: bouncing lightly on the balls of his feet with his hands tucked into his pockets.

"Hi," I say from the door, waiting for my stomach to complete its crazy Olly dance.

"Hey yourself." His voice is low and a little rough, sleep deprived.

"Thanks for chatting last night," he says, eyes tracking me all the way to the couch.

"Anytime." My own voice is husky and low as well. He looks paler than usual today and his shoulders are slumped forward a little, but still he's moving.

"Sometimes I wish I could just disappear and leave them," he confesses, ashamed.

I want to say something, not just something, but the *perfect* thing to comfort him, to make him forget his family for a few minutes, but I can't think of it. This is why people touch. Sometimes words are just not enough.

Our eyes meet and, since I can't hug him, I wrap my arms around my own waist, holding on tight.

His eyes drift across my face as if he's trying to remember

something. "Why do I feel like I've always known you?" he asks.

I don't know but I feel it, too. He stops moving, having come to whatever decision he needed to.

He says your world can change in a single moment.

He says no one is innocent, except maybe you, Madeline Whittier.

He says that his dad wasn't always this way.

CHAOS THEORY

TEN-YEAR-OLD OLLY AND his dad are at the breakfast bar in their old penthouse apartment in New York City. It's Christmastime, so maybe it's snowing outside, or maybe it just stopped snowing. This is a memory, so the details are a bit uncertain.

His dad has made fresh hot chocolate. He's a connoisseur and prides himself on making it from scratch. He melts actual bars of baking chocolate and uses whole "one hundred percent of the fat" milk. He takes Olly's favorite mug, pours in a layer of chocolate and adds six ounces of hot milk heated to almost boiling on the stove—never in the microwave. Olly stirs the milk and chocolate together while his dad gets the whipped cream, also freshly made, from the fridge. The cream is just lightly sweetened, the kind of sweet that makes you want more. He spoons one dollop, maybe two into Olly's mug.

Olly raises his cup and blows on the already melting whipped cream. It slides across the surface like a miniature iceberg. He eyes his dad over the top of the mug, trying to gauge what kind of mood he's in.

Lately the moods have been bad, worse than normal.

"Newton was wrong," his dad says now. "The universe is not deterministic."

Olly kicks his legs. He loves when his dad talks to him like this, "mano a mano," like he's a grown-up, even though he doesn't always understand what he's saying. They'd been having more of these conversations since his dad's suspension from work.

"What does that mean?" Olly asks.

His dad always waits for Olly to ask before explaining anything.

"It means one thing doesn't always lead to another," he says, and takes a slurp of hot chocolate. Somehow his dad never blows on the hot liquid first. He just dives right in. "It means you can do every *goddamn* thing right, and your life can still turn to shit."

Olly holds his sip of hot chocolate in his mouth and stares at his mug.

A few weeks ago Olly's mom had explained that his dad was going to be home for a while until things were fixed at his work. She wouldn't say what was wrong, but Olly had overheard words like "fraud" and "investigation." He wasn't quite sure what any of it meant, only that his dad seemed to love Olly and Kara and his mom a little less than he did before. And the less he seemed to love them, the more they tried to become more lovable.

The phone rings and his dad strides over to it.

Olly swallows his mouthful of hot chocolate and listens.

At first his dad uses his work voice, the one that's angry and relaxed at the same time. Eventually, though, his voice just turns to angry. "You're firing me? You just said those assholes were clearing me."

Olly finds himself getting angry, too, on behalf of his dad. He puts his mug down and slips off his stool.

His dad paces the length of the room. His face is a storm.

"I don't care about the *goddamn* money. Don't do this, Phil. If you fire me everyone's going to think—"

He stops moving and holds the phone away from his ear. He doesn't say anything for a long minute.

Olly stops moving, too, hoping that whatever Phil says next will fix everything.

"Jesus. You guys can't do this to me. No one's going to touch me after this."

Olly wants to go to his dad and tell him everything is going to be OK, but he can't. He's too afraid. He slips out of the room, taking his hot chocolate with him.

The first time Olly's dad gets afternoon drunk—violent drunk, yelling-at-the-top-of-his-lungs drunk, doesn't-remember-what-happened-the-next-day drunk—doesn't happen until a few months later. He'd been home all day, arguing with financial news shows on television. One of the anchors mentioned the name of his old company, and he raged. He poured whiskey into a tall glass and then added vodka and gin. He mixed them together with a long spoon until the mixture was no longer the pale amber color of the whiskey and looked like water instead.

Olly watched the color fade in the glass and remembered the day his dad got fired and how he'd been too afraid to comfort him. What if he had—would things be different now? What if?

He remembered how his dad had said that one thing doesn't always lead to another.

He remembered sitting at the breakfast bar and stirring the milk and chocolate together. How the chocolate turned white, and the milk turned brown, and how sometimes you can't unmix things no matter how much you might want to.

Find Z in the following equation:

$$X + Y = Z$$

Where X is unknown and unknowable,
and where Y is unknown and unknowable.

SIGNATURE _____

READ + UNDERSTOOD_____

A TALE OF TWO MADDYS

"YOUR MOTHER WANTS to know if I've noticed anything different about you lately," says Carla from across the living room.

I'm watching the first *Mission: Impossible* movie with Tom Cruise. He plays a superspy, Ethan Hunt, who leads a double, sometimes triple, and sometimes quadruple life. It's toward the end and Ethan has just unmasked himself, literally, to catch the bad guys.

Carla repeats herself, louder this time.

"And have you?" I ask as Ethan is pulling off his incredibly realistic mask to reveal his true face. I tilt my head to one side for a better perspective.

Carla grabs the remote from my hand and hits pause. She tosses the remote into the corner of the couch.

"What's wrong?" I ask, feeling guilty for ignoring her.

"It's you. And that boy."

"What do you mean?"

She sighs and sits. "I knew it was a mistake letting you two see each other."

She has my full attention now. "What did my mom say?"

"Did you cancel a movie night with her?"

I knew I shouldn't have done it. She looked so hurt and disappointed, but I didn't want to wait until after nine to IM with Olly. I can't get enough of talking to him. I'm overflowing with words. I'll never come to the end of all the things I want to say to him.

"And she says you're distracted all the time. And you ordered a lot of clothes. And shoes. And she almost beat you at some game that you always win."

Oh.

"Does she suspect?"

"That's all you're worrying about? Listen to what I'm telling you. Your mother is missing you. She's lonely without you. You should've seen her face when she was asking me."

"I just—"

"No," she says, holding a hand up. "You can't see him anymore." She picks up the discarded remote and clutches it in her hands, looking anywhere but at me.

Panic sends my heart racing. "Carla, please. Please don't take him away from me."

"He's not yours!"

"I know—"

"No, you don't know. He's not yours. Maybe he has time for you right now, but he's going to go back to school soon. He's going to meet some girl, and he's going to be *her* Olly. You understand me?"

I know she's just trying to protect me, just as I was trying to protect myself a few short weeks ago, but her words make me aware that the heart in my chest is a muscle like any other. It can hurt.

"I understand," I say quietly.

"Spend some time with your mother. Boys come and go, but mothers are forever."

I'm sure she's said these very same words to her Rosa.

"All right." She hands me back the remote. Together we watch the unmoving screen.

She pushes down on the tops of her knees with both hands and rises.

"Did you mean it?" I ask her when she's halfway across the room.

"Mean what?"

"You said that love couldn't kill me."

"Yes, but it might kill your mother." She manages a small smile.

I hold my breath, waiting.

"OK, fine. You can still see him, but you have to get some sense into you. You understand?"

I nod my agreement and turn the television off. Ethan Hunt vanishes.

I spend the rest of the day in the sunroom away from Carla. I'm not angry at Carla, but I'm not *not* angry either. All my doubts about keeping Olly a secret from my mom have vanished. I can't believe that one canceled date with her almost led to my not being able to see Olly again. Before, I was worried about keeping secrets from her. Now, I'm worried about not being able to have any secrets at all. I know she's not upset that I bought new clothes. She's upset that I didn't ask her opinion and bought them in colors that she didn't expect. She's upset with the change she didn't see coming. I resent and understand it at the same time. She's had to control so many things to keep me safe in my bubble.

And she's not wrong. I *have* been distracted when I'm with her, my mind constantly tuning into Radio Olly. I know she's not wrong. But still I resent it. Isn't growing apart a part of growing up? Don't I get to have even this bit of normalcy?

Even so, I feel guilty. She's devoted her entire life to me. Who am I to throw that away at the first sign of love?

Carla eventually finds me for our 4 p.m. checkup.

"Is there such a thing as sudden onset schizophrenia?" I ask.

"Why? You have it?"

"Maybe."

"Am I talking to good Maddy or bad Maddy right now?"

"Unclear."

She pats my hand. "Be good to your mama. You're all she has."

FREEDOM CARD

Email

COMPOSE

INBOX (4)
SENT MAIL
DRAFTS
TRASH
MORE ▾

We've received your credit card application

Argentis Inc.
to me ▾

Thank you for applying for your new Argentis
FreedomCard, the credit card that allows you
the flexibility and spending power to pursue
your dreams and plan for the future.

YOUR PERSONAL INFORMATION
Madeline F. Whittier
304 Papillon Way

ARGENTIS
FREEDOMCARD
1234 5678 9012 3456
YOUR NAME HERE

UPSIDE DOWN

NORMAL PEOPLE PACE when they're nervous. Olly stalks.

"Olly! It's just a handstand. Against a wall. I'll be fine." It's taken me an hour to convince him to show me how to do one.

"You don't have enough wrist or upper body strength," he grumbles.

"You used that one already. Besides, I'm strong," I say, and flex a single bicep. "I can bench-press my weight in books."

He smiles a little at that, then mercifully stops stalking. He flicks his rubber band as his eyes scan my body, mentally critiquing my lack of physical fortitude.

I roll my eyes as dramatically as possible.

"Fine," he sighs, with equal drama. "Squat." He demonstrates.

"I know what a—"

"Concentrate."

I squat down.

From across the room he checks my form and instructs me to make adjustments—hands twelve inches apart, arms straight with elbows pressed against my knees, fingertips splayed—until I'm just right.

"Now," he says, "shift your weight forward just slightly until your toes come off the ground."

I shift too far and roll head over heels onto my back.

"Huh," he says, and then presses his lips together. He's trying not to laugh, but the telltale dimple gives it away. I get back in position.

"More shift, less tilt," he says.

"I thought I was shifting."

"Not so much. OK, now. Watch me." He crouches down. "Hands twelve inches apart, elbows against your knees, fingertips splayed. Then slowly, slowly shift your weight forward onto your shoulders—get those toes off the ground—and then just push yourself up." He pushes up into the handstand with his usual effortless grace. Again I'm struck by how peaceful he is in motion. This is like meditation for him. His body is his escape from the world, whereas I'm trapped in mine.

"Do you want to see it again?" he asks, flowing back to his feet.

"Nope." Overeager, I push forward into my shoulder as instructed, but nothing happens. Nothing happens for about an hour. My lower half remains firmly anchored to the ground while my upper arms burn from the effort. I manage several more unintentional somersaults. By the end all I've gotten good at is not yelping as I roll over.

"Take a break?" he asks, still trying not to smile.

I growl at him, lower my head, and push forward again into another somersault. Now he's definitely laughing.

I remain flat on my back, catching my breath, and then I'm laughing along with him. A few seconds later I crouch back into a squat.

He shakes his head. "Who knew you were this stubborn?"

Not me. *I* didn't know I was this stubborn.

He claps his hands together. "OK, let's try something new. Close your eyes."

I close them.

"Good. Now, pretend you're in outer space."

With my eyes closed he feels closer, as if he's right next to me instead of across the room. His voice slides up my neck, whispers into my ear. "See the stars? And that asteroid field? And that lonely satellite going by? There's no gravity. You're weightless. You can do anything you want with your body. You just have to think it."

I tilt forward and suddenly I'm upside down. At first I'm not sure I've done it. I open and close my eyes a few times, but the world remains inverted. Blood rushes to my head, making me feel heavy and light-headed all at once. Gravity pulls my mouth into a smile and tugs my eyes open. I am wonderfully foreign in my own body. My upper arms begin to wobble. I overtilt from the vertical position and my feet touch the wall. I push off to reverse my direction and fall back into a crouch.

"Awesome," Olly says, clapping. "You even held it for a few seconds. Pretty soon you won't need the wall at all."

"How about now?" I say, wanting more, wanting to see the world the way he does.

He hesitates, about to argue, but then his eyes meet mine. He nods and crouches down to watch.

I squat, shift, and push up. I'm unstable almost immediately and begin to fall backward. Olly's suddenly right next to me, his hands on the bare skin of my ankles, holding me steady. Every nerve in my body migrates to where he touches. The skin under his hand sparks to life, every cell alight with feeling. I feel as if I've never been touched before.

"Down," I say, and he gently lowers my legs until they're back on the ground. I wait for him to move back to his corner, but he doesn't. Before I can think better of it, I stand up and face him. We're only three feet apart. I could reach out and touch him if I wanted to. I move my eyes slowly up to his.

"You OK?" he asks.

I mean to say yes, but I shake my head instead. I should move. He should move. He needs to go back to his side of the world, but he doesn't, and I can see in his eyes that he won't. My heart beats so loudly that I'm certain he can hear it.

"Maddy?" My name is a question and my eyes move to his lips.

He reaches out his right hand and grabs my left index finger. His hand is rough, uneven with calluses, and so warm. He rubs his thumb once across my knuckle and then cocoons my finger in the palm of his hand.

I look back down at my hand.

Friends are allowed to touch, right?

I disentangle my finger so that I can entangle all the others until our palms are pressed against each other.

I look back up to his eyes and see my reflection there. "What do you see?" I ask.

"Well, the first thing is those freckles."

"You're obsessed."

"Slightly. It looks like someone sprinkled chocolate across your nose and cheeks." His eyes travel down to my lips and back up to my eyes. "Your lips are pink and they get pinker when you chew on them. You chew on them more when you're about to disagree with me. You should do that less. The disagreeing, not the chewing. The chewing is adorable."

I should say something, stop him, but I can't speak.

"I've never seen anyone with hair as long and poofy and curly as yours is. It looks like a cloud."

"If clouds were brown," I say, finally finding my voice, trying to break the spell.

"Yes, curly brown clouds. And then your eyes. I swear they change color. Sometimes they're almost black. Sometimes they're brown. I'm trying to find a correlation between the color and your mood, but I don't have it yet. I'll keep you posted."

"Correlation is not causation," I say, just to have something to say.

He grins and squeezes my hand. "What do you see?"

I want to answer, but I find that I can't. I shake my head and look back down at our hands.

We remain that way, sliding between certainty and uncertainty and back again until we hear Carla's approach and are forced to part.

I am made. I am unmade.

SKIN

I READ ONCE that, on average, we replace the majority of our cells every seven years. Even more amazing: We change the upper layers of our skin every two weeks. If *all* the cells in our body did this, we'd be immortal. But some of our cells, like the ones in our brains, don't renew. They age, and age us.

In two weeks my skin will have no memory of Olly's hand on mine, but my brain will remember. We can have immortality or the memory of touch. But we can't have both.

FRIENDSHIP

Later, 8:16 P.M.

Olly: you're logged on early

Madeline: I told my mom I had a lot of homework.

Olly: are you all right?

Madeline: Are you asking if I'm sick?

Olly: yes

Madeline: So far, so good.

Olly: are you worried?

Madeline: No. I'm fine.

Madeline: I'm sure I'm fine.

Olly: you are worried

Madeline: A little.

Olly: i shouldn't have. i'm sorry

Madeline: Please don't be. I'm not. I wouldn't trade it.

Olly: still

Olly: are you sure you're ok?

Madeline: I feel brand-new.

Olly: all from holding hands huh. imagine what a kiss would do

Madeline: . . .

Madeline: Friends don't kiss, Olly.

Olly: really good ones can

RESEARCH

TWENTY-FOUR HOURS LATER, kissing is all I think about. I
see the words *imagine what a kiss would do* whenever I close my
eyes. At some point it occurs to me that I don't know anything
about kissing. Of course, I've read about it. I've seen enough
kissing in movies to get the idea. But I've never pictured myself
as a kiss*ee*, and certainly not a kiss*er*.

Carla says we're probably OK to see each other again today, but
I decide to wait a couple more days. She doesn't know about
the touch on my ankle, the holding hands, the almost-shared
breath. I should tell her, but I don't. I'm afraid she'll stop our
visits. Another lie to add to my growing count. Olly's now the
only person in my life that I haven't lied to.

Forty-eight hours post-touch and I'm still feeling fine. I sneak
peeks at my charts when Carla's not looking. Blood pressure,
pulse, and temperature all seem OK. No early warning signs
in sight.

My body goes a little haywire when I imagine kissing Olly,
but I'm pretty sure that's just lovesickness.

Pre-kiss checklist

☑ Lip balm

☑ Review potential hand positions

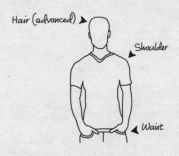

Hair (advanced) ▶

◀ Shoulder

◀ Waist

Practice kissing technique

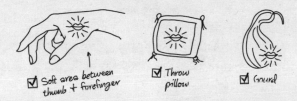

☑ Soft area between thumb + forefinger

☑ Throw pillow

☑ Gourd

SIGNATURE _____

READ + UNDERSTOOD _____

Creating the correct kissing atmosphere

Rain

Proven to heighten passion

See: "The Notebook"

"Four Weddings + a Funeral"

A portable audio device

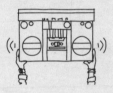

Provides properly swelling music

See: Almost every rom-com, ever

An epic love poem

To be memorized + recited just prior to the kiss act

SIGNATURE _____

READ + UNDERSTOOD_____

Kiss Mechanics

Ensure probability of kissing

extended

eye contact

unnecessary touching

Pucker lips to correct degree of firmness

well done

Jell-O

too firm   too soft

Tilt head to prevent nose collisions

30°

Lean in

Partner will make up remaining distance

Make contact

Press and hold for 3-5 seconds

Pull back slowly

Note: keep eyes closed!

SIGNATURE _____

READ + UNDERSTOOD_____

LIFE AND DEATH

OLLY'S NOT ON the wall. He's not even at a far end of the couch. Instead, he's right in the middle, elbows on knees, stretching and releasing his rubber band.

I hesitate in the doorway. His eyes don't leave my face. Does he feel the same urge to occupy the same space, to breathe the same air that I do?

I linger at the threshold to the room, uncertain. I could go to his traditional spot next to the wall. I could stay right here in the doorway. I could tell him that we shouldn't push my luck, but I can't. More than that, I don't want to.

"I think orange is your color," he says finally.

I'm wearing one of my new T-shirts. It's V-necked and close fitting and, now, my most favorite piece of clothing. I may buy ten more of this exact shirt.

"Thanks." I lay a hand across my stomach. The butterflies are back and restless.

"Should I move?" He stretches the rubber band taut between his thumb and index finger.

"I don't know," I say.

He nods and begins to rise.

"No, wait," I say, pressing my other hand to my stomach and walking over to him. I sit, leaving a foot of space between us.

He lets the rubber band snap against his wrist. His shoulders release a tension I didn't realize he'd been holding.

Next to him, I press my knees together, hunch my shoulders. I make myself as small as possible, as if my size could belie our closeness.

He lifts his arm from his knee, holds his hand out, and wiggles his fingers.

All my hesitation vanishes and I slip my hand into his. Our fingers slide into position as if we've been holding hands like this all our lives. I don't know how the distance between us closes.

Did he move? Did I?

Now we're next to each other, thighs touching, forearms warm against each other, my shoulder pressing into his upper arm. He rubs his thumb across mine, tracing a path from knuckle to wrist. My skin, each individual cell, lights up. Normal, nonsick people get to do this all the time? How do they survive the sensation? How do they keep from touching *all the time*?

He tugs my hand just slightly. It's a question, I know, and I look up from the miracle of our hands to the miracle of his face and eyes and lips moving closer to mine. Did I move? Did he?

His breath is warm and then his lips are brushing butterfly-soft against mine. My eyes close on their own. The romantic comedies are right about this part. You have to close your eyes. He pulls away and my lips are cold. Am I doing it wrong? My eyes fly open and crash into the darkening blue of his. He kisses me like he's afraid to continue and he's afraid to stop. I grip the front of his shirt and hold on tight.

My butterflies are rioting.

He squeezes my hand and my lips part and we're tasting each other. He tastes like salted caramel and sunshine. Or what I think salted caramel and sunshine taste like. He tastes like nothing I've ever experienced, like hope and possibility and the future.

I pull away first this time, but only because I need air. If I could, I would kiss him every second of every day for all the days.

He leans his forehead against mine. His breath is warm against my nose and cheeks. It's slightly sweet. The kind of sweet that makes you want more.

"Is it always like that?" I ask, breathless.

"No," he says. "It's *never* like that." I hear the wonder in his voice.

And just like that, everything changes.

HONESTLY

Later, 8:03 P.M.

Olly: no movie night with your mom?

Madeline: I canceled. Carla's going to be upset with me.

Olly: why?

Madeline: I promised her I would spend more time with my mom.

Olly: i'm messing up your life

Madeline: No, please don't think that.

Olly: what we did today was crazy

Madeline: I know.

Olly: what were we thinking?

Madeline: I don't know.

Olly: maybe we should take a break?

Madeline: ...

Olly: sorry. i'm trying to protect you

Madeline: What if protection is not what I need?

Olly: what does that mean?

Madeline: I don't know.

Olly: i need you to be safe. i don't want to lose you

Madeline: You barely have me!

Madeline: Are you sorry?

Olly: for what? for kissing?

Olly: honestly?

Madeline: Of course.

Olly: no

Olly: are you sorry?

Madeline: No.

OWTSYD

THE UNIVERSE AND my subconscious may be conspiring against me. I'm in the den playing Fonetik with my mom. So far in tonight's game I've gotten tiles to play *OWTSYD*, *FRIDUM*, and *SEEKRITS*. That last one nets me a bonus for using all seven letters. She frowns down at the board and I think she's going to challenge my word, but she doesn't. She tallies the score and, for the first time ever, I'm actually winning. I'm ahead of her by seven points.

I look down at the score and then back at her. "Are you sure you did that right?" I ask. I don't want to beat her on top of everything else.

I tally the score to find that she's right.

Her eyes are on my face, but I keep staring at the scorecard. She's been like this all night, watchful, as if I'm a puzzle to be worked out. Or maybe I'm being paranoid. Maybe it's the guilt I feel for being so selfish, for wanting to be with Olly even now. Every moment I spend with him I learn something new. I become someone new.

She takes the scorecard from my hands and lifts my chin so that I have to meet her eyes. "What's going on, honey?"

I'm about to lie to her when there's a sudden high scream

from outside. Another scream follows and then indistinct yelling and a loud slam. We both spin to stare at the window. I start to rise, but my mom presses down on my shoulder, shakes her head. I let her hold me in place, but another scream of "STOP" has both of us running to the window.

The three of them—Olly, his mom, and his dad—are on the porch. Their bodies form a triangle of misery, fear, and anger. Olly's in fighter stance, fists clenched, feet planted wide and firm. Even from here I can see veins bulging to the surface of his arms, his face. His mom takes a step toward Olly, but he says something to her that makes her retreat.

Olly and his dad face off. His dad is holding a drink in his right hand. He doesn't take his eyes off Olly as he lifts and finishes it with deep gulps. He holds the empty glass out for Olly's mom to take. She starts to move, but, again, Olly says something to stop her. His dad turns to look at her then, his hand still rigidly holding the glass. For a moment I think that maybe she won't go to him.

But her defiance doesn't last. She takes a step toward him. He grabs at her, all anger and menace. But Olly's suddenly right there in between them. He swats his dad's arm away and pushes his mom off to the side.

Even angrier now, his dad lunges again. Olly shoves him backward. He bangs into the wall, but doesn't fall.

Olly begins dancing lightly on his feet, shaking out his arms and wrists like a boxer preparing for a bout. He's trying to draw his dad's attention away from his mom. It works. His dad lunges at him fist first. Olly dodges right and then left. He hops backward down the porch steps just as his dad swings again. His dad misses, and momentum sends him tripping down the steps. He lands in a sprawl on the concrete driveway and doesn't move.

Olly grows still. His mom claps both hands over her mouth. My mom wraps an arm around my shoulder. I press my forehead to the glass and grip the windowsill. All of our eyes are on his dad. The moment stretches out. Every second he doesn't move is a terrible relief.

His mom is the first to break. She hurries down the steps, crouches down next to him, runs her hand down his back. Olly gestures for her to get away, but she ignores him. She leans in closer just as his dad flips over onto his back. He snatches her wrist in his big, cruel hands. Face triumphant, he hoists her hand up in the air like it's a trophy that he's won. He pulls himself to standing and drags her up with him.

Again, Olly rushes between them, but this time his dad is ready. Quicker than I've ever seen him move, he lets go of Olly's mom, grabs the collar of Olly's shirt, and punches him in the stomach.

His mom screams. Then I'm screaming, too. He punches him again.

I don't see what happens next because I pull away from my mom and I'm running. I don't think; I just move. I fly out of the room and down the hall. I'm through the air lock and out the door in no time at all.

I don't know where I'm going, but I have to get to him.

I don't know what I'm doing, but I have to protect him.

I sprint across our grass to the edge of the lawn closest to

Olly's house. His father is lunging for him again when I scream, "STOP!"

They both freeze momentarily in place and look at me, shocked. His dad's drunkenness catches up to him. He stumbles back up the steps and into the house. His mom follows.

Olly bends over, holding his stomach.

"Are you all right?" I ask.

He looks up at me, his face morphing from pain to confusion to fear.

"Go. Go back," he says.

My mom grabs my arm and tries to pull me away. I'm vaguely aware that she's hysterical. She's stronger than I would've thought, but my need to see Olly is stronger.

"Are you all right?" I cry out again, unmoving.

He straightens up slowly, gingerly, like something hurts, but the pain doesn't show on his face.

"Mads, I'm OK. Go back. Please." The full weight of our feeling for each other hangs between us.

"I promise I'm OK," he says again, and I let myself be pulled away.

We're back in the air lock before I start to recognize what I've done. Did I really just go Outside? My mom's hand is a vise on my upper arm. She forces me to face her.

"I don't understand," she says, her voice shrill and confused. "Why would you do that?"

"I'm OK," I say, answering the question she doesn't ask. "It was only a minute. Less than a minute."

She relinquishes my arm and lifts my chin.

"Why would you risk your life for a total stranger?"

I'm not a skillful enough liar to hide my feelings from her. Olly's in my skin.

She sees the truth. "He's not a stranger, is he?"

"We're just friends. Online friends," I say. I pause. "I'm sorry. I wasn't thinking. I just wanted to make sure he was OK."

I rub my hands down my forearms. My heart beats so fast it hurts. The enormity of what I've done overwhelms me and I'm trembling.

My sudden shaking derails my mom's questioning and sends her into doctor mode. "Did you touch anything?" she asks, over and over again.

I tell her no, over and over again.

"I had to trash your clothes," she says after I've taken the shower that she insisted I take. She doesn't look at me as she says it. "And we're going to have to be extra careful for the next few days to make sure nothing's—"

She breaks off, unable to say the words.

"It was less than a minute," I say, for both our benefit.

"Sometimes a minute is all it takes." Her voice is almost not there at all.

"Mom, I'm sorry—"

She holds up a hand and shakes her head. "How could you?" she asks, finally meeting my eyes.

I'm not sure if she's asking about my going Outside or lying to her. I don't have an answer for either question.

*

As soon as she leaves, I go to the window in search of Olly, but I don't find him. He's probably on the roof. I get into bed.

Was I really just Outside? What did the air smell like? Was there wind? Did my feet even touch the ground? I touch the skin on my arms, my face. Is it different? Am I?

My entire life I've dreamed about being in the world. And now that I have, I don't remember any of it. Just the sight of Olly doubled over in pain. Just his voice telling me to go back.

THE THIRD MADDY

I'M ALMOST ASLEEP that night when my door opens. My mom hovers in the doorway and I keep my eyes closed, pretending to be asleep. Still, she comes in and sits on the bed next to me.

For a long time she doesn't move. Then she leans over and I'm sure she's going to kiss my forehead like she used to when I was a little girl, but I roll away from her, still feigning sleep.

I don't know why I do it. Who is this new Maddy that is cruel for no reason? She gets up, and I wait to hear the door close before opening my eyes.

A single black rubber band sits on my nightstand.

She knows.

LIFE IS A GIFT

THE NEXT MORNING I wake to yelling. At first I think it's Olly's family again, but the sound is too close. It's my mom. I've never heard her voice raised before.

"How could you do this? How could you let a stranger in here?"

I can't hear Carla's response. I open the bedroom door quietly and tiptoe out onto the landing. Carla's standing at the foot of the stairs. My mom is smaller than her in every way, but you wouldn't know it from the way Carla's shrinking away from her.

I can't let Carla get blamed for this. I fly down the stairs.

"Did something happen? Is she sick?" Carla catches my arm, pats my face, her eyes scanning my body for signs of trouble.

"She went outside. Because of him. Because of *you*." She turns to face me. "She put her life at risk and she's been lying to me for weeks."

She turns back to Carla. "You're fired."

"No, please, Mom. It wasn't her fault."

She cuts me off with a hand. "Not *only* her fault, you mean. It was your fault, too."

"I'm sorry," I say, but it has no effect on her.

"So am I. Carla, pack your things and go."

I'm desperate now. I can't imagine my life without Carla in it. "Please, Mom, please. It won't happen again."

Time with Mom.

New neighbors.

Something to think about.

A special night.

Olly.

Maddy & Carla.

Watching Olly.

Hawaii.

Heart-to-heart.

Olly & Maddy.

The bookshop.

Together.

"Of course it won't." She says it with absolute certainty.

Carla starts up the stairs without a word.

Mom and I spend the next half hour watching Carla pack. She has reading glasses and pens and clipboards in almost every room.

I don't bother to wipe away my tears because they just keep coming. Mom holds herself more rigid than I've ever seen her. When we finally get to my room I give Carla my copy of *Flowers for Algernon*. She looks at me and smiles.

"Isn't this book going to make me cry?" she asks.

"Probably."

She pulls the book close to her bosom and holds it there and doesn't take her eyes off me.

"You be brave now, Madeline." I run into her arms. She drops her medical bag and the book and holds me tight.

"I'm so sorry," I whisper.

She squeezes me even tighter. "It's not your fault. Life is a gift. Don't forget to live it." Her voice is fierce.

"That's enough now," my mom snaps from the doorway. Her patience has run out. "I know this is very sad for you both. Believe it or not, it's sad for me as well. But it's time for you to go. Now."

Carla lets me go. "Be brave. Remember, life is a gift." She picks up her medical case.

We all walk downstairs together. Mom hands her a final check, and she's gone.

MADELINE'S DICTIONARY

as•ymp•tote (ˈasəm(p)ˌtōt) *n. pl.*
-s. 1. A wish that continually
approaches but never achieves
fulfillment. [2015, *Whittier*]

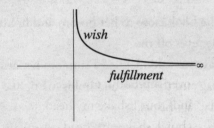

MIRROR IMAGE

I PULL THE curtains aside as soon as I'm back in my room. Olly's standing at his window, his forehead pressed into his fist, his fist pressed into the glass. How long has he been waiting? It takes him a second to realize I'm there, but it's enough time for me to see his fear. Evidently my function in life is to strike fear into the hearts of those who love me.

Not that Olly loves me.

His eyes roam over my body, my face. He makes a typing gesture with his hands, but I shake my head. He frowns, makes the gesture again, but I shake my head again. He disappears from the window and returns with a marker.

R U OK?

I nod. *Are you?* I mouth.

YES. I'M?

I shake my head.

GROUNDED?

I nod.

NO INTERNET?

I nod.

HOW LONG?

I shrug.

SURE YOU'RE OK?

I pantomime excellent health, existential angst, regret, and an enormous sense of loss, all via a single nod.

We stare mutely at each other.

I'M SORRY?

I shake my head. A gesture that says: *No, don't be sorry. It's not your fault. It's not you. It's this life.*

SCHEDULE CHANGE

Sun	Mon	Tue	Wed	Thu	Fri	Sat
	Mom home on vacay	◎	*NU RSE Inter views* ← →		FFnite dinner croque monsieur	Nurse inter views
More nurse inter views	Nurse Ritchett's first day			◎	FFnite dinner soupe à l'oignon	

notes

145

MORE THAN THIS

MY MOM WORDLESSLY kneels to gather scraps of drawings from our game of Honor Pictionary and stacks them into a neat pile. She keeps the best (defined here as either really good or really bad) ones from each game. We sometimes look through our collection nostalgically, the way other families look through old photos. Her fingers linger atop a particularly bad drawing of some sort of horned creature hovering above a circle with holes in it.

She holds the drawing up for me to see. "How did you guess 'nursery rhyme' from this?" She chuckles with effort, trying to break the ice.

"I don't know," I say, and laugh, wanting to meet her halfway. "You are a terrible drawer."

The creature was supposed to be a cow and the circle was supposed to be the moon. Truly, my guess was inspired, given how awful her drawing was.

She pauses stacking for a moment and sits back on her heels. "I really had a good time with you this week," she says.

I nod but don't say anything back. Her smile fades. Now that Olly and I can't see or talk to each other, my mom and I spend more time together. It's the only good thing to come out of this mess.

I reach out and grab her hand, squeeze it. "Me too."

She smiles again, but less fully now. "I hired one of the nurses."

I nod. She offered to let me interview Carla's potential replacements, but I declined. It doesn't matter who she hires. No one's ever going to be able to replace Carla.

"I have to go back to work tomorrow."

"I know."

"I wish I didn't have to leave you."

"I'll be OK."

She straightens the already perfectly straight stack of drawings. "You understand why I have to do the things I'm doing?" Besides firing Carla, she's also revoked my Internet privileges and canceled my in-person architecture lesson with Mr. Waterman.

We've mostly avoided talking about this all week. My lies. Carla. Olly. She took the week off from work and tended to me in Carla's absence. She took my vitals every hour instead of every two and slumped with relief each time the results were normal.

By day four she said we were out of the woods. We got lucky, she said.

"What are you thinking?" she asks.

"I miss Carla."

"I do, too, but I'd be a bad mother if I let her stay. Do you understand? She put your life in danger."

"She was my friend," I say quietly.

The anger that I'd been expecting from her all week finally sparks.

"But she wasn't just your friend. She was your nurse. She was supposed to keep you safe. She wasn't supposed to endanger your life or introduce you to teenage boys who are going to break your heart. Friends don't give you false hope."

I must look as stricken as I feel, because she suddenly stops and wipes her palms down the front of her thighs. "Oh, baby girl. I'm so sorry."

And that's when it really hits me and all at once. Carla's really gone. She won't be here tomorrow when my mom leaves for work. Instead, it will be someone new. Carla's gone, and it's my fault. And Olly's gone, too. I won't ever get a chance at kiss number two. I gasp against the pain of the thought, against the end of something barely even begun.

I'm sure my mom will eventually allow me access to the Internet and we'll be able to IM again, but it won't be enough. If I'm honest with myself, I'll admit that it was never going to be enough.

I'll never get to the end of all the ways I want to be with him. She presses her hand against her own heart. I know we're feeling the same pain.

"Tell me about him," she says.

I've wanted to tell her about him for so long, but now I'm not sure where to begin. My heart is so full of him. So, I begin at the beginning. I tell her about seeing him for the first time, about the way he moves—light and fluid and certain. I tell her about his ocean eyes and calloused fingers. I tell her how he's less cynical than he thinks he is. About his awful dad, about his dubious wardrobe choices.

I tell her that he thinks I'm funny and smart and beautiful

in that order, and that the order matters. All the things I've wanted to say for weeks. She listens and holds my hand and cries along with me.

"He sounds wonderful. I see why you think so."

"He is."

"I'm sorry that you're sick."

"It's not your fault."

"I know, but I wish that I could give you more than this."

"Can I have my Internet privileges back?" I have to try.

She shakes her head. "Ask me for something else, honey."

"Please, Mom."

"It's better this way. I don't want you to have a broken heart."

"Love can't kill me," I say, parroting Carla's words.

"That's not true," she says. "Whoever told you that?"

NURSE EVIL

MY NEW NURSE is an unsmiling despot with a nursing degree. Her name is Janet Pritchert. "You may call me *Nurse* Janet," she says. Her voice is unnaturally high, like an alarm.

She emphasizes the word *Nurse* so that I understand that simply calling her Janet will not do. Her handshake is too firm, as if she's more used to crushing things than caring for them.

It's possible that my view of her is biased.

All I see when I look at her is how much she's not Carla. She's thin where Carla was stout. Her speech is not peppered with Spanish words. She has no accent at all. Compared with Carla, she's altogether *less*.

By the afternoon I've decided to adjust my attitude, but that's when the first of her notes appears, stickied to my laptop.

DAILY PRESCRIPTIVES™
FROM THE DESK OF

Janet Pritchert, RN

DON'T FORGET!
Rules are not meant to be broken!

NOTES:

NO Internet after 3 p.m.

My mom has reinstated my Internet access but only during the school day. She says I'm only supposed to be using it for schoolwork, but I'm sure the fact that Olly has started school and only gets home after 3 P.M. has something to do with it.

I check the time. It's 2:30 P.M. I decide not to adjust my attitude. Nurse Janet could've at least given me a chance to break the rule before assuming that I would be a rule breaker.

Things don't improve the next day:

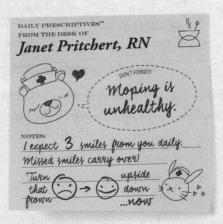

Over the next week, I give up any hope I had that she could be persuaded to my cause. Her mission is clear—monitor, contain, and control.

Olly and I settle into a new rhythm. We IM in short bursts during the day in between my Skype classes. At 3 P.M., Nurse Evil turns off the router and our communication ends. At night, after dinner and after my mom and I spend time with each other, Olly and I stare at each other out the window.

I plead with my mom about the rule, but she refuses to budge. She says it's for my own protection.

The next day Nurse Evil finds another reason to leave me a note:

I stare at the note, remembering that Carla had said the same thing as she was leaving: *Life is a gift.* Am I wasting mine?

NEIGHBORHOOD WATCH #2

OLLY'S SCHEDULE

   6:55 AM — Stands at window. Writes GOOD MORNING on the glass.

   7:20 AM — Waits for Kara to finish her cigarette.

   7:25 AM — Leaves for school.

   3:45 PM — Returns home from school.

   3:50 PM — Stands at window. Erases GOOD MORNING and writes HI on glass.

   9:05 PM — Stands at window. Writes a few questions.

   10:00 PM — Writes GOODNIGHT MADDY on the glass.

MADDY'S SCHEDULE

   6:50 AM — Waits for Olly to appear at window.

   6:55 AM — Is joyful.

   7:25 AM — Despairs.

   8:00 AM–3:00 PM —Ignores Nurse Evil. Attends classes. Does homework. Reads. Compulsively checks for IM messages. Reads some more.

   3:40 PM — Watches for Olly's car to arrive.

   3:50 PM — Is joyful.

4:00 PM – More homework. More reading.
6:00 PM–9:00 PM – Dinner/hang out with Mom.
9:01 PM – Waits for Olly to appear at window.
9:05 PM – Is joyful. Pantomimes answers to questions.
10:01 PM – Despair, cont'd.

HIGHER EDUCATION

WITH OLLY BACK in school, our IM sessions are even more limited. He IMs when he can—in between classes or, sometimes, right in the middle of one. During his first week back he does his best to make me feel as if I'm right there with him. He sends pictures of his locker (#23), his class schedule, the library and the librarian, who looks exactly as I imagine a high school librarian would, which is to say bookish and wonderful. He sends pictures of math proofs from his AP math class, his AP English required reading list, pictures of beakers and petri dishes from his biology and chemistry classes.

I spend that first week—and it does feel like spending, like not seeing him is costing me something—doing all my normal things: reading, learning, not dying. I write alternate titles for the books on his reading list. *A Tale of Two Kisses. To Kiss a Mockingbird. As I Lay Kissing.* And so on.

Nurse Evil and I settle into a grudging routine where I pretend she doesn't exist and she leaves ever more obnoxious sticky notes to let me know that she does.

But it's not just about missing him. I'm also jealous of his life, of his world that expands beyond his front door.

He tells me that high school is no utopia, but I'm not convinced. What else would you call a place that exists solely to teach you about the world? What do you call a place with friends and teachers and libraries and book club and math club and debate club and any other kind of club and after-school activities and endless possibilities?

By the third week it becomes harder to sustain our relationship in this new form. I miss *talking* to him. You can only pantomime so much. I miss being in the same room with him, his physical presence. I miss the way my body was always aware of his. I miss getting to know him. I miss getting to know the Maddy that I am when I'm with him.

We continue like this until, finally, the inevitable happens.

I'm standing at the window as his car pulls up. I wait for him to exit, to wave our customary wave, but he doesn't get out first.

A girl that is not Kara emerges from the back of the car.

Maybe she's a friend of Kara's.

But then Kara slams out of the car and into the house, leaving Olly and Mystery Girl alone. Mystery Girl laughs at something Olly says. She turns, puts her hand on his shoulder, and smiles at him the way I've smiled at him.

I'm shocked at first, not quite believing what my eyes are seeing. Is she touching *my* Olly? My stomach clenches. I'm being squeezed around the middle by a giant hand. My organs are displaced until I feel *wrong* inside my own skin.

I let the curtain fall and duck away from the window. I feel like a Peeping Tom.

My mom's words come back to me. *I don't want you to have a broken heart.* She knew what would happen. There was always going to be someone else. Someone who isn't sick. Someone who can leave her house. Someone he can talk to and touch and kiss and everything else.

I stifle the urge to go back to the window and assess my competition. But it's not a competition if one person can't even show up for the event. And it doesn't matter what she looks like. It doesn't matter if she's long- or short-legged. It doesn't matter if she's pale or tanned, if her hair is black or brown or red or blond. It doesn't matter if she's pretty or not.

It matters that she feels the sun on her skin. She breathes unfiltered air. It matters that she lives in the same world that Olly does, and I don't. I never will.

I take another peek. Her hand is still on his shoulder and she's still laughing. He's frowning up at my window, but I'm sure he can't see me. He waves anyway, but I duck down again, pretending to both of us that I'm not there.

ALOHA MEANS HELLO
AND GOOD-BYE, PART ONE

I'VE CANCELED YET another mother-daughter night, so my mom stops by my room.

"So," she says.

"I'm sorry I canceled, Mom. I'm just feeling out of sorts."

She immediately presses the back of her hand to my forehead.

"Mentally, not physically," I clarify. I can't get the image of Mystery Girl's hand on Olly's shoulder out of my head.

She nods but doesn't remove her hand until she's satisfied that I'm not feverish.

"So," I say, prompting her. I really do want to be alone.

"I was a teenager once. And an only child. I was very lonely. I found being a teenager to be very painful."

This is why she's here? Because she thinks I'm lonely? Because she thinks I'm having some sort of teenage *angst*?

"I am not lonely, Mom," I snap. "I am alone. Those are different things."

She flinches but doesn't retreat. Instead, she lets go of whatever she is holding and caresses my cheek until I meet her eyes.

"I know, baby girl." Her hands are behind her back again. "Maybe now is not a good time. Do you want me to go?"

She's always so reasonable and understanding. It's hard to be angry with her.

"No, it's OK. I'm sorry. Stay." I pull my legs up, making room for her. "What are you hiding?" I ask.

"I brought you a present. I thought it would make you feel less lonely, but now I'm not so sure."

She pulls a framed photograph from behind her back. My heart squeezes inside my chest. It's an old photograph of the four of us—me, my mom and dad and brother—standing on a beach, someplace tropical. The sun has set behind us and who-ever took the picture used the flash and so our faces are bright, almost glowing, against the darkening sky.

My brother is holding on to my dad with one hand and clutching a small brown stuffed bunny rabbit with the other. For the most part he's a miniature version of my mom with her same straight black hair and dark eyes. Really the only difference is that he has my dad's darker skin. My dad's wearing a matching Aloha-print shirt and shorts. *Goofy* is the only word I can think of to describe him. Still, he's so handsome. His arm is wrapped around my mom's shoulder and he seems to be pulling her closer. He's staring straight into the camera. If ever there was someone who had everything he wanted, my dad was him.

Mom is wearing a red, strapless, flower-patterned sundress. Her damp hair curls around her face. She's not wearing makeup or jewelry. Really, she looks like an alternate-universe version of the mom sitting next to me now. She seems to belong on that beach with those people more than she belongs stuck here in this room with me. She's holding me in her arms, and she's the only one not staring into the camera. Instead, she's laughing at me. I'm grinning that silly, gummy smile that only babies can smile.

I've never seen a photo of myself Outside before. I didn't know such a thing existed.

"Where's this?" I ask.

"Hawaii. Maui was your dad's favorite place."

Her voice is almost a whisper now. "You were just four months old, before we knew why you were always sick. A month before the accident."

I clutch the photo to my chest. My mom's eyes fill with tears that don't fall.

"I love you," she says. "More than you know."

But I do know. I've always felt her heart reaching out to protect mine. I hear lullabies in her voice. I can still feel arms rocking me to sleep and her kisses on my cheeks in the morning. And I love her right back. I can't imagine the world she's given up for me.

I don't know what to say, so I tell her I love her, too. It's not enough, but it'll have to do.

After she leaves I stand in front of the mirror holding the photograph next to my face. I look from the me in the photo to the me in the mirror and back again.

A photograph is a kind of time machine. My room fades away, and I'm on that beach surrounded by love and salt air and the fading warmth and lengthening shadows of sunset.

I fill my tiny lungs with as much air as they can take and I hold my breath. I've been holding it ever since.

LATER, 9:08 P.M.

OLLY'S ALREADY WAITING for me when I go to the window.
In big, bold letters he writes:

ЯƎИTЯAꟼ BA⅃

I pantomime my complete and utter lack of jealousy.

MADAM, I'M ADAM

SOMETIMES I REREAD my favorite books from back to front. I start with the last chapter and read backward until I get to the beginning. When you read this way, characters go from hope to despair, from self-knowledge to doubt. In love stories, couples start out as lovers and end as strangers. Coming-of-age books become stories of losing your way. Your favorite characters come back to life.

If my life were a book and you read it backward, nothing would change. Today is the same as yesterday. Tomorrow will be the same as today. In the *Book of Maddy*, all the chapters are the same.

Until Olly.

Before him my life was a palindrome—the same forward and backward, like "A man, a plan, a canal. Panama," or "Madam, I'm Adam." But Olly's like a random letter, the big bold *X* thrown in the middle of the word or phrase that ruins the sequence.

And now my life doesn't make sense anymore. I almost wish I hadn't met him. How am I supposed to go back to my old life, my days stretching out before me with unending and brutal sameness? How am I supposed to go back to being The Girl

Who Reads? Not that I begrudge my life in books. All I know about the world I've learned from them. But a description of a tree is not a tree, and a thousand paper kisses will never equal the feel of Olly's lips against mine.

THE GLASS WALL

A WEEK LATER, something startles me awake. I sit up. My head is foggy with sleep but my heart is awake and racing. It knows something that my head doesn't yet know.

I glance at the clock. 3:01 A.M. My curtains are closed, but I can see a glow from Olly's room. I drag myself over to the window and push aside the curtains. His entire house is ablaze with lights. Even the porch light is on. My hearts speeds up even more.

Oh, no. Are they fighting again?

A door slams. The sound is faint but unmistakable. I gather the curtains in my fist and wait, willing Olly to show himself. I don't wait for long because just then he stumbles onto the porch as if he's been pushed.

The urge to go to him fills me up like it did the last time. I want to go to him. I *need* to go to him, to comfort him, to protect him.

He regains his balance with his usual speed and spins to face the door with fists clenched. I brace along with him for an attack that doesn't come. He remains in fighter stance, facing the door, for a full minute. I've never seen him so still.

Another minute passes and then his mom joins him on the porch. She tries to touch his arm but he jerks away and doesn't even look at her. Eventually she gives up. As soon as she's gone, all the tension leaves his body. He presses the heels of his hands into his eyes and his shoulders begin to shake. He looks up to my window. I wave, but he doesn't respond. I realize he can't see me because my lights are off. I run to the switch. But by the time I return to the window, he's gone.

I press my forehead, my palms, my forearms against the glass.

I've never wanted out of my skin more.

THE HIDDEN WORLD

SOMETIMES THE WORLD reveals itself to you. I'm alone in the darkening sunroom. Late-afternoon sun cuts a trapezoid of light through the glass window. I look up and see particles of dust drifting, crystal white and luminous, in the suspension of light.

There are entire worlds that exist just beneath our notice of them.

HALF LIFE

IT'S A STRANGE thing to realize that you're willing to die. It doesn't come in a flash, a sudden epiphany. It happens slowly, a balloon leak in reverse.

The sight of Olly crying alone on his porch will not leave me.

I pore over the pictures that he sent from school. I make myself a place in every single one. Maddy in the library. Maddy standing next to Olly's locker waiting to go to class. Maddy as Girl Most Likely To.

I memorize every inch of my family photo, trying to divine its secrets. I marvel at the not-sick Maddy, baby Maddy, her life stretching before her with endless possibility.

Ever since Olly came into my life there've been two Maddys: the one who lives through books and doesn't want to die, and the one who *lives* and suspects that death will be a small price to pay for it. The first Maddy is surprised at the direction of her thoughts. The second Maddy, the one from the Hawaii photograph? She's like a god—impervious to cold, famine, disease, natural and man-made disasters. She's impervious to heartbreak.

The second Maddy knows that this pale half life is not really living.

GOOD-BYE

Dear Mom,

The first thing is that I love you. You already know that, but I may not get the chance to tell you again.

So. I love you. I love you. I love you.

You are smart and strong and kind and selfless. I couldn't have wished for a better mom.

You're not going to understand what I'm going to say. I don't know if I understand it myself.

Because of you I'm alive, Mom, and I'm so, so grateful for that. Because of you I've survived this long and gotten a chance to know my small part of the world. But it's not enough. It's not your fault. It's this impossible life.

I'm not doing this just because of Olly. Or maybe I am. I don't know. I don't know how to explain it. It's Olly and it's not-Olly at the same time. It's like I can't look at the world in the old way anymore. I found this new part of myself when I met him and the new part doesn't know how to stay quiet and still and just observe.

Do you remember when we read <u>The Little Prince</u> together for the first time? I was so upset that he died in the end. I didn't understand how he could choose death just so he could get back to his rose.

I think I understand it now. He wasn't choosing to die. His rose was his whole life. Without her, he wasn't really alive.

I don't know, Mom. I don't know what I'm doing, only that I have to. Sometimes I wish I could go back to the way I was before, before I knew anything. But I can't.

I'm sorry. Forgive me. I love you.

- Maddy

THE FIVE SENSES

HEARING

The alarm's keypad tries to announce my escape by emitting a loud *BEEP* each time I press a number. I can only hope that the sound is too unexpected and my mom's room too far away from the door for her to hear it.

The door unseals with a sigh.

I'm Outside.

The world is so quiet it roars.

TOUCH

The front-door handle is metal-cool and smooth, almost slippery. It's easy to let go of it, and I do.

SIGHT

It's 4 A.M. and too dark for detail. My eyes take in only the general shape of things, fuzzy silhouettes against the night sky. Large tree, smaller tree, steps, garden, stone path leading to a gate with a picket fence on either side. Gate, gate, gate.

SMELL

I'm in Olly's garden. The air is full, ripe with scent—flowers, earth, my expanding fear. I store it away in my lungs. I toss pebbles at his window, willing him to come out.

TASTE

Olly's in front of me, stunned. I don't say anything. I press my lips to his. At first he's frozen, uncertain and unyielding, but then he's not. All at once, he pulls me tight against him. One of his hands is in my hair and the other one is gripping my waist.

He tastes just like I remember.

OTHER WORLDS

WE COME TO our senses.

Well, Olly comes to his. He pulls away, grips my shoulders with both hands. "What are you doing out here? Are you all right? Is something wrong? Is your mom OK?"

I'm all bravado. "I'm fine. She's fine. I'm running away."

The light from his room above casts just enough light so I can see confusion across the planes of his face.

"I don't understand," he says.

I take a deep breath, but freeze midway.

The night air is cold and moist and heavy and completely unlike any air I've ever breathed.

I try to *un*breathe it, to expel it from my lungs. My lips tingle and I'm light-headed. Is that just fear, or is it something else?

"Maddy, Maddy," he whispers against my ear. "What have you done?"

I can't answer. My throat is blocked like I've swallowed a stone.

"Try not to breathe," he says, and starts guiding me back to my house.

I let him pull me for a second, maybe two, but then I stop moving.

"What is it? Can you walk? Do you need me to carry you?"

I shake my head and pull my hand from his.

I take a sip of night air. "I said I'm running away."

He makes a sound like a growl. "What are you talking about? Do you have a death wish?"

"Opposite," I say. "Will you help me?"

"With what?"

"I don't have a car. I don't know how to drive. I don't know anything about the world."

He makes another sound halfway between a growl and a laugh. I wish I could see his eyes in the dark.

Something slams. A door? I grab his hands and pull us both flat against the side of his house. "What was that?"

"Jesus. A door. From my house."

I press myself flatter against the wall, trying to disappear. I peek over to the path leading from my house, fully expecting to see my mother coming down it. But she's not there.

I close my eyes. "Take me to the roof."

"Maddy—"

"I'll explain everything."

My entire plan hangs on him helping me. I didn't really consider what would happen if he refused.

We are quiet for one breath. And then two. And then three.

He takes my hand and guides me around to the side of his house farthest from mine. There's a tall ladder leading to the roof.

"Are you afraid of heights?" he asks.

"I don't know." I start climbing.

I duck down as soon as we get to the roof, but Olly says there's no need.

"Most people don't look up anyway," he says.

It takes a few minutes for my heart to return to normal.

Olly folds himself down with his usual unusual grace. I'm happy to watch him move.

"So, what now?" he asks after a time.

I look around. I'd always wanted to know what he did up here. The roof is gabled in parts, but we're sitting on a flat section toward the back. I make out shapes: a small wooden table with a mug, a lamp, and some crumpled papers. Maybe he writes up here, composes bad poetry. Limericks.

"Does that lamp work?" I ask.

He wordlessly turns it on, and it casts a diffuse circle of light around us. I'm almost afraid to look at him.

The crumpled papers on the table are fast-food wrappers. Not a secret poet, then. Next to the table there's a dusty gray tarp covering something, or somethings. The ground is littered with tools—wrenches, wire cutters in various sizes, hammers, and a few others that I don't recognize. There's even a blowtorch.

I finally look over at him.

His elbows are on his knees and he's staring out at the slowly brightening sky.

"What do you *do* up here?" I ask.

"That can't possibly matter right now." His voice is hard and he doesn't look at me. There's no trace of the boy who kissed me so desperately a few minutes ago. His fear for me has crowded everything else out.

Sometimes you do things for the right reasons and sometimes for the wrong ones and sometimes it's impossible to tell the difference.

"I have pills," I say.

He's barely moving as it is, but now he grows completely still. "What pills?"

"They're experimental, not FDA-approved. I ordered them online. From Canada." The lie is easy, effortless.

"Online? How do you know they're even safe?"

"I did a lot of research."

"But still, you can't be sure—"

"I'm not reckless." I hold his eyes. These lies are for his own protection. Already he looks relieved.

I press on. "They should give me a few days outside. I didn't tell my mom because she wouldn't want to risk it, but I—"

"Because it's risky. You just said they're not FDA—"

"They're safe enough for a few days." My tone holds no doubt. I wait, hoping that he will swallow the lie.

"Jesus." He drops his face into his hands and holds it there. When he looks up, it's a less obstinate Olly staring back at me. Even his voice softens. "You could have told me this five minutes ago."

I make my best effort to lighten the mood. "We were kissing! And then you were getting angry with me." I'm blushing from the talk of kissing and from my easy lying. "I was going to tell you. I am telling you. I just did."

He's much too smart to fall for this, but he wants it to be true. He wants it to be true more than he wants the truth. The smile that breaks across his face is cautious, but so beautiful that I can't look away. I would lie to him again for that smile.

"Now," I say. "What's under that thing?"

He hands me a corner of the tarp and I pull it aside.

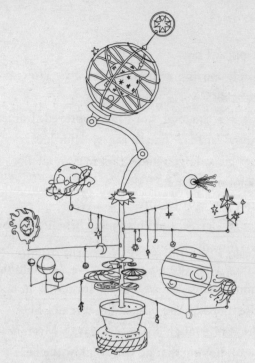

At first I'm not sure what I'm looking at. It's like reading a seemingly random collection of words before the sentence becomes clear.

"It's beautiful," I say.

"It's called an orrery."

"This is what you've been doing up here? Making universes?"

He shrugs.

A small wind blows and the planets spin slowly. We both watch their motion without speaking.

"Are you sure about this?" Doubt has crept back into his voice.

"Please help me, Olly. Please." I point to the orrery. "I need to escape, too, just for a little while."

He nods. "Where do you want to go?"

ALOHA MEANS HELLO
AND GOOD-BYE, PART TWO

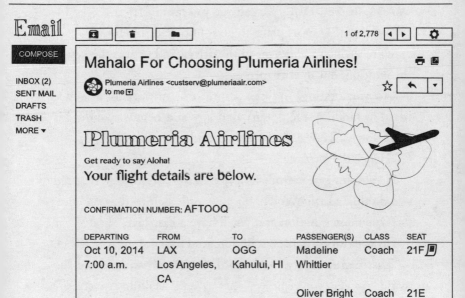

Email

COMPOSE

INBOX (2)
SENT MAIL
DRAFTS
TRASH
MORE ▼

Mahalo For Choosing Plumeria Airlines!

Plumeria Airlines <custserv@plumeriaair.com>
to me ▼

Plumeria Airlines

Get ready to say Aloha!

Your flight details are below.

CONFIRMATION NUMBER: AFTOOQ

DEPARTING	FROM	TO	PASSENGER(S)	CLASS	SEAT
Oct 10, 2014 7:00 a.m.	LAX Los Angeles, CA	OGG Kahului, HI	Madeline Whittier	Coach	21F
			Oliver Bright	Coach	21E

HAPPY ALREADY

"MADS, BE SERIOUS. We can't go to Hawaii."

"Why not? I got us plane tickets. I booked us a hotel."

We're sitting in Olly's car in the driveway. He puts the key in the ignition, but doesn't turn it.

"Are you kidding?" he asks, scrutinizing my face for evidence that I'm kidding. He doesn't find any and begins shaking his head slowly. "Hawaii is three thousand miles away."

"Hence the airplane."

He ignores my attempt at levity. "You're serious? When did you do this? How? Why?"

"One more question and you'll have a Fast Five," I say.

He leans forward, presses his forehead into the steering wheel.

"Last night, with a credit card, because I want to see the world."

"You have a credit card?"

"I got my own a few weeks ago. There are perks to hanging out with an older woman."

He pulls his forehead off the wheel, but still stares straight ahead not meeting my eyes. "What if something happens to you?"

"Nothing will."

"But what if it does?"

"I have the pills, Olly. They're going to work."

He squeezes his eyes shut and puts his hand on the key. "You know, we have plenty of world right here in southern California."

"But no humuhumunukunukuapuaa."

A small half smile forms at the corner of his lips. I need to make it spread across his entire face.

He turns to face me. "What are you talking about?"

"The humuhumunukunukuapuaa."

"What is a humu-whatever?"

"The state fish of Hawaii."

His smile broadens. "Of course it is." He turns the key in the ignition. His eyes linger on his house and his smile fades, just slightly. "How long?"

"Two nights."

"OK." He grabs my hand and gives it a quick kiss. "Let's go see this fish."

Olly's mood gets better, lighter somehow, the farther away from his house that we get. This trip gives him the perfect excuse to let go of the burden of his family for a little while, at least. Also, an old friend of his from New York, Zach, lives in Maui.

"You'll love him," he tells me.

"I'll love everything," I respond.

Our flight's not until 7 A.M. and I have a detour I want to make.

Being in his car is like being in a very loud, very fast-moving bubble. He refuses to open the windows. Instead, he presses a button on the dashboard that prevents air circulation. The sound of the tires on asphalt is like someone hissing low and constant into my ears. I fight the urge to cover them.

Olly says we're not going very fast, but to me we're hurtling through space. I've read that passengers on high-speed trains say that the world outside the train blurs from the speed. I know we're not going anywhere near that fast. But still, the landscape moves too quickly for my slow eyes to hold on to. I barely catch glimpses of houses in the brown hills in the distance. Overhead signs with cryptic symbols and writing come and go before I can decipher them. Bumper stickers and license plates appear and disappear in a blink.

Even though I understand the physics of it, I find it strange that my body could be moving though I am sitting still. Well, not exactly still. I'm pushed backward into my seat whenever Olly accelerates and I lurch forward whenever he brakes.

Every so often we slow down enough and I can see other people in their cars.

We pass a woman shaking her head and slapping at the steering wheel with her hands. Only after we've passed her do I figure out that she was probably dancing to music. Two kids in the back of another car stick their tongues out at me and laugh. I don't do anything because I'm not sure what the etiquette is for that.

Gradually we slow down to a more human speed and leave the highway.

"Where are we?" I ask.

"She lives in Koreatown."

My head buzzes from trying to look everywhere at once. There are brightly lit signs and billboards written only in

Korean. Since I can't read the language, the signs seem like art pieces with beautiful, mysterious forms. Of course, they probably just say things as mundane as *Restaurant* or *Pharmacy* or *Open 24 Hours*.

It's early, but still there are so many people doing so many things—walking or talking or sitting or standing or running or riding bicycles. I don't quite believe they're really real. They're just like the mini figures I pose in my architecture models, here to give Koreatown the *vigor of life*.

Or maybe it's me that's not really real, not really here at all.

We drive along for a few minutes more. Eventually we pull up to a two-story apartment complex with a fountain in the courtyard.

Olly undoes his seat belt but makes no move to leave the car. "Nothing can happen to you," he says.

I reach over and take his hand. "Thank you," is all I can think to say. I want to tell him that it's his fault that I'm out here. That love opens you up to the world.

I was happy before I met him. But I'm alive now, and those are not the same thing.

INFECTED

CARLA SCREAMS AND covers her face when she first sees me.

"Are you a ghost?" She grabs my shoulders, squeezes me against her bosom, rocks me side to side, and then squeezes me again. I don't have any air left in my lungs when she's finished.

"What are you doing here? You can't be here," she says, still squeezing me.

"I'm happy to see you, too," I squeak.

She pulls away, shakes her head as if I were some kind of a miracle, and pulls me back in for more.

"Oh, my girl," she says. "Oh, how I missed you." She holds my face in her hands.

"I missed you, too. I'm so sorry about—"

"Stop. You don't have anything to be sorry for."

"You lost your job because of me."

She shrugs. "I got another one. Besides, it's you that I miss."

"I miss you, too."

"Your mama did what she had to do."

I don't want to think about my mom. So I look around for Olly, who's standing off in the distance.

"You remember Olly," I say.

"How could I forget that face? And that body," she says, definitely loud enough for him to hear. She marches over to him and pulls him into a hug only slightly more restrained than the one she gave me.

"You taking care of our girl?" She pulls away and pats him a little too hard on his cheek.

Olly rubs it. "I'm doing my best. I don't know if you know this, but she can be a little stubborn."

Carla looks back and forth between us for a long second, noting the tension between us.

We're still standing in her doorway.

"Come inside. Come inside," she says.

"We didn't think you would be awake so early," I say as we enter.

"You stop sleeping when you get old. You'll see."

I want to ask, *Will I ever grow old?* But instead I ask, "Is Rosa here?"

"Upstairs, asleep. You want me to wake her?"

"We don't have time. I just wanted to see you."

She takes my face into her hands again and re-examines me, this time with nurse's eyes.

"I must've missed a lot of things. What are you doing here? How are you feeling?"

Olly steps closer, wanting to hear my answer. I wrap my arms around my stomach.

"I'm great," I say, far too brightly.

"Tell her about the pills," Olly says.

"What pills?" Carla demands, looking only at me.

"We got pills. Experimental ones."

"I know your mama didn't give you anything experimental."

"I got them on my own. Mom doesn't know."

She nods, validated. "From where?"

I tell her the same thing I told Olly, but she doesn't believe me. Not for a second. She covers her mouth with her hand and her eyes are cartoon big.

I put my heart into my eyes and plead with her silently. *Please, Carla. Please understand. Please don't expose me. You said life is a gift.*

She looks away and rubs small circles into a spot above her bosom.

"You must be hungry. I'll make you some breakfast."

She directs us to sit on a bright yellow overstuffed couch before disappearing into the kitchen.

"This is exactly the way I pictured her house," I say to Olly as soon as she's gone. I don't want him asking any questions about the pills.

Neither of us sits. I move a step or two away from him. The walls are painted in primary colors. Knickknacks and photos cover almost every surface.

"She seems OK with the pills," Olly says finally. He moves closer, but I tense up. I'm afraid he'll be able to feel the lies on my skin.

I wander around the living room, looking at photos of generations of women who all look like Carla. An enormous one of her holding Rosa when she was a baby hangs over a love seat. Something about the photo reminds me of my mom. It's the way she's looking at Rosa with not only love, but a kind of fierceness, too, like she would do anything to protect her. I'll never be able to repay her for all she's done for me.

Carla makes us a breakfast of *chilaquiles*—corn tortillas with salsa and cheese and *crema Mexicana*, which is something like crème fraîche. It is delicious and new, but I only have a single bite. I'm too nervous for food.

"So, Carla. In your professional opinion, do you really think the pills are working?" Olly asks. His voice is overflowing with optimism.

"Maybe," she says, but shakes her head as she says it. "I don't want to give you false hope."

"Tell me," I say. I need to ask her why I'm not sick yet, but I can't. I'm trapped by my lies.

"It could be the pills are delaying your sickness. Even without any pills, it could be you just haven't met any of your triggers yet."

"Or it could be that the pills are working," Olly says. He's moved beyond hope. As far as he's concerned these pills are a miracle.

Carla pats Olly's hand from across the table. "You're a good egg," she tells him.

She avoids looking at me and takes our plates and goes to the kitchen.

I follow behind her, shame making me slow. "Thank you."

She dries her hands on a towel. "I understand you. I understand why you're out here."

"I might die, Carla."

She wets a dishcloth and wipes down an already clean spot on the counter. "I left Mexico in the middle of the night with nothing. I didn't think I was going to survive. A lot of people don't make it, but I left anyway. I left my father and my mother and my sister and my brother."

She rinses the cloth, continues. "They tried to stop me. They said it wasn't worth my life, but *I* said that it was *my* life, and it was up to me to decide what it was worth. I said I was going to go and either I was going to die or I was going to get a better life."

Now she rinses the cloth again and wrings it tight. "I tell you, when I left my house that night I never felt more free. Even now, in all the time that I've been here, I never felt as free as that night."

"And you don't regret it?"

"Of course I regret it. A lot of bad things happened on that trip. And when my mother and father died, I couldn't go back for the funerals. Rosa doesn't know anything about where she's from." She sighs. "You're not living if you're not regretting."

What am I going to regret? My mind cycles through visions: my mom alone in my white room wondering where everyone she's ever loved went. My mom alone in a green field staring down at my grave and my dad's grave and my brother's grave. My mom dying all alone in that house.

Carla touches my arm and I force all the images ruthlessly from my head. I cannot bear to think about these things. If I do, I won't be able to live.

"Maybe I won't get sick," I whisper.

"That's right," she says, and hope spreads through me like a virus.

TTYL

FIRST-TIME FLYER FAQ

Q: What is the best way to relieve earaches caused
    by changes in cabin pressure?

A: Chewing gum. Also, kissing.

Q: Which is the best seat: window, center, or
    aisle?

A: Window, definitely. The world is quite a sight
    from 32,000 feet above it. Note that a window
    means your traveling companion may then be
    stuck next to a spectacularly loquacious bore.
    Kissing (your companion, not the bore) is also
    effective in this situation.

Q: How many times per hour is cabin air
    refreshed?

A: Twenty.

Q: How many people can an airline blanket
    comfortably cover?

A: Two. Be sure to raise the seat arm between you
    and snuggle as close as possible for maximum
    coverage.

Q:	How is it possible that humans invented
	something as amazing as an airplane and
	something as awful as a nuclear bomb?
A:	Human beings are mysterious and paradoxical.

Q:	Will I encounter turbulence?
A:	Yes. Into all lives a little turbulence must
	fall.

THE CAROUSEL

"I'VE DECIDED BAGGAGE carousels are a perfect metaphor for life," Olly says from atop the edge of a nonmoving one.

Neither of us has any checked luggage. All I'm carrying is a small backpack with essentials—toothbrush, clean underwear, *Lonely Earth Maui* guidebook, and *The Little Prince*. Of course I had to take it with me. I'm going to read it one more time to see how the meaning's changed.

"When did you decide this?" I ask.

"Just now." He's in a crackpot-theory mood, just waiting for me to ask him to elaborate.

"Want to give it some more thought before you regale me?" I ask.

He shakes his head and jumps down right in front of me. "I'd like to begin the *regaling* now. Please."

I gesture magnanimously for him to continue.

"You're born. You get thrown onto this crazy contraption called life that just goes around and around."

"People are the luggage in this theory?"

"Yes."

"Go on."

"Sometimes you fall off prematurely. Sometimes you get so

190

damaged by other pieces of luggage falling on your head that you don't really function anymore. Sometimes you get lost or forgotten and go around forever and ever."

"What about the ones that get picked up?"

"They go on to lead unextraordinary lives in a closet somewhere."

I open and close my mouth a few times, unsure where to begin.

He takes this as agreement. "See? It's flawless." His eyes are laughing at me.

"Flawless," I say, meaning him and not the theory. I thread my fingers through his and look around. "Does it look like you remember?" Olly's been here once before, on a family vacation when he was ten.

"I don't really remember much. I remember my dad saying it wouldn't kill them to spend a little money on first impressions."

The terminal is dotted with greeters—Hawaiian women in long, flower-patterned dresses holding welcome signs and strands of purple-and-white-orchid leis draped over their forearms. The air does not smell like the ocean. It smells industrial, like jet fuel and cleaning products. It's a smell I could come to love because it would mean that I was traveling. All around us the noise level rises and falls, punctuated by choruses of *alohas* sung out by greeters and families alike. As first impressions go, this one isn't bad. I wonder how his dad has managed to live in the world all his life without knowing what was precious in it.

"In your baggage theory, your mom is one of the bags that gets damaged?"

He nods.

"And your sister? She's one of the ones that gets lost, goes around and around forever?"

He nods again.

"And you?"

"Same as my sister."

"And your dad?"

"He's the carousel."

I shake my head. "No," I say, and grab his hand. "He doesn't get to have everything, Olly."

I've embarrassed him. He tugs his hand out of mine, moves a small distance away, studies the terminal.

"You, my dear, need a lei," he says. He nods at a greeter who hasn't yet found her party.

"I don't," I say.

"Oh, but you do," he insists. "Wait here." He makes his way over to her. At first she shakes her head no, but Olly persists, as he's wont to do. A few seconds later they're both looking over at me. I wave to prove to her that I'm nice and friendly, the sort of person you might want to give a free lei to.

She relents. Olly comes back triumphant. I reach out to take it, but he places it over my head instead.

"You know, leis were traditionally given only to royalty," I say, quoting from my guidebook. He gathers my hair into his hands and caresses the back of my neck before letting the lei fall into place.

"Who doesn't know that, princess?"

I finger the strand, feeling as if the lei has transferred some of its beauty to me.

"Mahalo nui loa," I say. "It means *thank you very much.*"

"You read every single word in that guidebook, didn't you?"

I nod my head. "If I had a suitcase," I say, "I would love it. I would shrink-wrap it when I traveled. I would put stickers from every place I'd ever been on it. And when I saw it on the carousel I would grab it with both hands and I'd be so happy to have it because then my adventures could really begin."

He looks at me, a nonbeliever confronted with, if not evidence, then at least the possibility of God. He pulls me into his arms and we're wrapped around each other, his face buried in my hair and my face pressed into his chest, no daylight between our bodies.

"Don't die," he says.

"I won't," I say back.

MADELINE'S DICTIONARY

prom•ise (ˈprämɒs) *n.* *pl.* **-es.**
1. The lie you want to keep.
[2015, *Whittier*]

HERE NOW

ACCORDING TO THE guidebook, Maui is shaped like a head. Our cab ride will take us across the neck, along the jawline, over the chin, mouth, nose, and up to the wide forehead. I've booked us into a hotel in Ka'anapali, which is in the skull just beyond the hairline, geographically speaking.

We turn a corner and suddenly the ocean is just there, running alongside the road to the left of us. It can't be more than thirty feet away.

The vast endlessness of it is shocking. It falls off the end of the world.

"I can't believe I've missed all this," I say. "I've missed the whole wide world."

Olly shakes his head. "One thing at a time, Maddy. We're here now."

I look back at Olly's ocean eyes and I'm drowning, surrounded on all sides by water. There's so much to see that it's hard to know what to pay attention to. The world is too big and there's not enough time for me to see it.

Again he reads my mind. "Do you want to stop and look?"

"Yes, please."

He asks the driver if it's OK for us to pull over, and he says it's no problem at all. He knows a good place coming up, a park and picnic area.

I'm out of the car before the engine's off. The water is just a short walk downhill and then across the sand.

Olly trails a distance behind me.

The ocean.

It's bluer, bigger, more turbulent than I'd imagined. Wind lifts my hair, scrubs sand and salt against my skin, invades my nose. I wait until I'm down the hill to take off my shoes. I roll my jeans up as far as they'll go. The sand is hot and dry and loose. It waterfalls over my feet and slips through my toes.

As I get closer to the water, the sand changes. Now it sticks to my feet, coating them like a second skin. At the water's edge, it changes again and becomes a liquid velvet. My feet leave impressions in this softer mix.

Finally, my feet are in the surging water, and then my ankles are, and then my calves. I don't stop moving until the water is up to my knees and soaks my jeans.

"Be careful," Olly calls out from somewhere behind me.

I'm not sure what that means in this context. Be careful because I may drown? Be careful because I may get sick? Be careful because once you become a part of the world it becomes a part of you, too?

Because there's no denying it now. I'm in the world.

And, too, the world is in me.

MADELINE'S DICTIONARY

o•cean (ˈōSHən) *n. pl.* **-s. 1.** The endless part of yourself you never knew but always suspected was there. [2015, *Whittier*]

REWARD IF FOUND

OUR HOTEL SITS right on the beach and we can see and smell the ocean from the small open-air lobby. We're greeted with *alohas* and more leis. Olly gives his to me so that I now have three layered around my neck. A bellhop in a bright yellow-and-white Hawaiian shirt offers to retrieve our nonexistent luggage. Olly makes a noise about our baggage coming later and steers us around him before he can question us further.

I nudge Olly toward the check-in counter and give him our paperwork.

"Welcome to Maui, Mr. and Mrs. Whittier," says the woman at the desk. He doesn't correct her mistake, just pulls me closer and gives me a loud smack on the lips.

"Mahalo very much," he says, grinning wildly.

"You'll be joining us for . . . two nights."

Olly looks to me for confirmation and I nod.

A few keystrokes later the woman tells us that, though it's still early, our room is already ready. She gives us a key and property map and tells us about the complimentary continental breakfast buffet.

"Enjoy your honeymoon!" She winks and sends us on our way.

*

The room is small, very small, and decorated much like the lobby, with teak furniture and large pictures of bright tropical flowers. Our balcony—called a *lanai*—overlooks a small garden and a parking lot.

From the center of the room, I turn a 360 to see what's considered necessary in a temporary home—television, a small fridge, an enormous closet, a desk and chair. I turn another 360 trying to figure out what's missing.

"Olly, where are our beds? Where do we sleep?"

He looks momentarily confused until he spots something. "Oh, you mean this?" He walks over to what I thought was an enormous closet, grips the two handles near the top and pulls to reveal a bed. "Voilà," he says. "The very model of modern-day, space-saving efficiency. The height of style and comfort, of convenience and practicality. I give you the Murphy bed."

"Who is Murphy?" I ask, still surprised that a bed came out of the wall.

"The inventor of this bed," he says, winking.

With the bed unfolded, the room feels even smaller. We both stare at it for longer than is strictly necessary. Olly turns to look at me. I'm blushing even before he says:

"Just the one bed." His voice is neutral, but his eyes aren't. The look in his eyes makes me blush harder.

"So," we say simultaneously. We laugh awkward, self-conscious laughs and then laugh at ourselves for being so very awkward and self-conscious.

"Where is that guidebook?" he asks, finally breaking eye

contact and making a show of looking around the room. He grabs my backpack and digs around, but pulls out *The Little Prince* instead of the guide.

"I see you brought the essentials," he teases, waving it in the air. He climbs onto the bed and begins lightly bouncing in the middle of it. Murphy's springs protest noisily. "Isn't this your favorite book of all time?"

He turns the book over in his hands. "We read this sophomore year. I'm pretty sure I didn't understand it."

"You should try again. The meaning changes every time you read it."

He looks down at me. "And how many times have you—"

"A few."

"More or less than twenty?"

"OK, more than a few."

He grins and flips open the front cover. "Property of Madeline Whittier." He turns to the title page and continues reading. "Reward if Found. A visit with me (Madeline) to a used bookstore. Snorkel with me (Madeline) off Molokini to spot the Hawaiian state fish."

He stops reading aloud, continues silently instead. "When did you write this?" he asks.

I start to climb onto the bed, but stop when the room sways a little. I try again and another wave of vertigo unbalances me.

I turn and sit, facing away from him. My heart squeezes so painfully in my chest that it takes my breath away.

Olly's immediately at my side. "Mad, what is it? What's wrong?"

Oh, no. Not yet. I'm not ready. "I'm light-headed," I say. "And my stomach—"

"Do we need to go to a hospital?"

My stomach growls loud and long in reply.

I look up at him. "I think I'm—"

"Hungry," we say simultaneously.

Hunger.

That's what I'm feeling. I'm not getting sick. I'm just hungry.

"I'm starving," I say. In the last twenty-four hours I've had a single bite of *chilaquiles* and a handful of Nurse Evil's apple slices.

Olly starts laughing. He collapses backward onto the bed. "I've been so worried that something in the air was gonna kill you." He presses the heels of his hands to his eyes. "Instead you're going to starve to death."

I've never actually been this hungry before. For the most part I've always eaten my three meals and two snacks exactly on time every day. Carla was a big believer in food. *Empty tummy, empty head*, she'd say.

I lie back and laugh along with him.

My heart squeezes again, but I ignore it.

REMEMBRANCE OF THINGS PRESENT

I FEEL MUCH better after we grab a quick bite to eat. We need beach gear and, according to Olly, souvenirs, so we stop in a store called, helpfully, Maui Souvenir Shop and General Store. I don't think I've ever seen so much stuff. I find myself overwhelmed with the sheer volume of it. Stacks and stacks of T-shirts and hats that say *Maui*, or *Aloha*, or some variation of that. Racks of hanging flower-patterned dresses in almost every color. Carousel after carousel of tchotchkes—key chains, shot glasses, magnets. One carousel is dedicated solely to surfboard key chains with stenciled names, alphabetically arranged. I search for Oliver or Madeline or Olly or Maddy, but don't find any.

Olly comes up behind me and wraps a single arm around my waist. I'm standing in front of a wall of calendars featuring shirtless surfers. They're not unattractive.

"I'm jealous," he murmurs into my ear, and I laugh and rub my hands over his forearm.

"You should be." I reach for one of the calendars.

"You're not really—"

"For Carla," I say.

"Sure, sure."

"What did you get?" I lean my head back against his chest.

"Seashell necklace for my mom. Pineapple ashtray for Kara."

"Why do people buy all this stuff?"

He holds me a little tighter. "It's not so mysterious," he says. "It's so we remember to remember."

I turn in his arms, thinking how quickly it's become my favorite place in the world. Familiar, foreign, comforting, and thrilling all at once.

"I'm going to get this for Carla," I say, brandishing the calendar. "And chocolate-covered macadamia nuts. And one of those dresses for myself."

"What about your mom?"

What kind of memento do you get for the mother who has loved you your whole life, who has given up the world for you? Who you may never see again? Nothing will ever do, not really.

I think back to the old photograph she showed me of all of us in Hawaii. I have no memory of it, no memory of being on that beach with her and my dad and my brother, but she does. She has memories of me, of a life that I don't have at all.

I pull away from Olly and wander around the store. By eighteen years old, other teenagers have separated from their parents. They leave home, have separate lives, make separate memories. But not me. My mom and I have shared the same closed space and breathed the same filtered air for so long that it's strange being here without her. It's strange making memories that don't include her.

What will she do if I don't make it home? Will she gather

her memories of me close? Will she take them out and examine them and live them over and over again?

I want to give her something of this time, of my time without her. Something to remember me by. I find a carousel with vintage postcards and I tell her the truth.

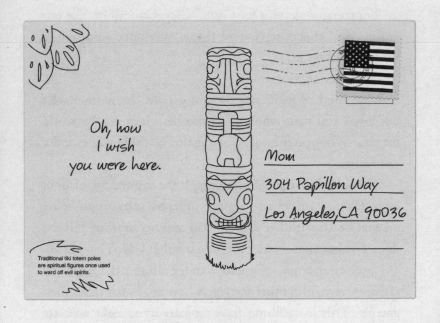

Oh, how
I wish
you were here.

Mom
304 Papillon Way
Los Angeles, CA 90036

Traditional tiki totem poles
are spiritual figures once used
to ward off evil spirits.

THE SWIMSUIT

IT'S POSSIBLE THAT I should've tried on the swimsuit before I bought it. It's not that it doesn't fit. It's that it does, and very closely. Am I really expected to appear in public with so little clothing on?

I'm in the bathroom looking between my actual body and my body in the mirror. The suit is a bright pink one-piece with spaghetti straps. The pink is so bright that it gives color to my cheeks. I look flushed, like a rosy-cheeked summer girl who belongs in the sun.

Humidity has made my hair bigger than normal. I gather it up and plait it into a long braid to subdue it. I look back to the mirror. The only way to subdue this suit is to wear more, possibly all my clothing at once. I scan my body again. There's really no denying that I have breasts and legs in this thing. All my parts seem to be in the right proportion and in the right place. I twist a little to confirm that my derriere is covered, and it is, but only just. What would I see in the mirror if I were a normal girl? Would I think that I was too fat or too thin? Would I dislike my hips, my waist, my face? Would I have body-image issues? As it stands, my only issue is that I would gladly trade this body for one that works properly.

Olly knocks on the door. "Are you snorkeling in there?"

I do eventually have to leave this bathroom, but I'm too nervous. Will Olly think all my parts are in the right place?

"Deep-sea fishing actually." My voice shakes only slightly.

"Fantastic. We'll have sushi for—"

I pull the door open quickly, like ripping off a Band-Aid.

Olly just stops talking. His eyes travel slowly from my face to my toes and even more slowly back up again.

"You're in a swimsuit," he says. His eyes are on the expanse of skin between my neck and chest.

"I am." I look up into his eyes and what I see there makes me feel like I'm not wearing any clothing at all. My heart picks up the pace and I take a deep breath to try to slow it down, but it doesn't work.

He runs his hands along the length of my arms, slowly pulling me toward him at the same time. He touches his forehead to mine when we're finally close enough. His eyes are blue fire.

He looks like a starving man, like he could devour me all at once.

"That swimsuit," he begins.

"Is small," I conclude.

GUIDE TO HAWAIIAN REEF FISH

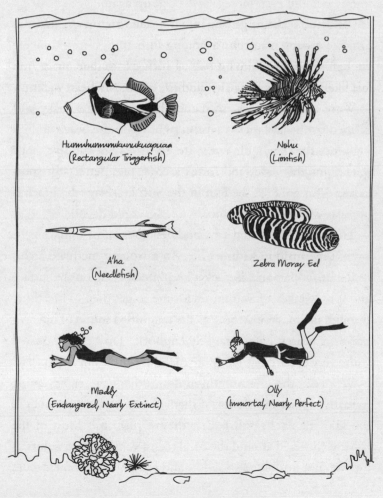

Humuhumunukunukuapuaa
(Rectangular Triggerfish)

Nohu
(Lionfish)

A'ha
(Needlefish)

Zebra Moray Eel

Maddy
(Endangered, Nearly Extinct)

Olly
(Immortal, Nearly Perfect)

JUMP

I SURPRISE OLLY by getting into the water right away. He says I'm like a baby who runs headlong into things, not knowing enough to be afraid. Like a baby, I stick my tongue out at him and make my way, life jacket and all, farther into the water.

We're at Black Rock, so named because of the rocky cliff formed by the lava rocks that run right up to the beach and jut high into the sky. In the water, the rocks form a crescent shape that calms the waves and forms a coral reef perfect for snorkeling. Our guide at the Fun in the Sun desk says the beach is popular with cliff divers, too.

The water is cold and salty and delicious and I think maybe I was a mermaid in a former life. An astronaut mermaid architect. The flippers and life jacket keep me floating on the surface and it only takes a few minutes for me to get used to breathing through the mask. Listening to the magnified sound of my own breath is peaceful and strangely euphoric. I'm being reassured with every breath that I'm more than just alive. I'm living.

We see the humuhumunukunukuapuaa right away. Actually, we see quite a lot of them. I guess the reason they're the Hawaiian state fish is that they're plentiful. Most of the fish are clustered around the coral reef. I've never seen colors so intense, not just blue and yellow and red, but the deepest blues and brightest yellows and most vibrant reds you've ever seen. Away from the coral, the sun's rays form rectangular columns of light in the water. Schools of silver fish dart in and out, acting with one mind.

Holding hands, we swim farther out and see gliding stingrays that look like giant white-bellied birds. We see two enormous sea turtles that seem to be flying instead of swimming. Intellectually I know that they won't hurt us. But they're so big, and so obviously belong to this water world—where I do not— that I stop moving, not wanting to attract their attention.

I could stay all day, but Olly eventually tugs me back to shore. He doesn't want us, meaning me, to get burned by the midday sun.

Back on the beach we dry off under a shady tree. I feel Olly's eyes on me when he thinks I'm not noticing, but we are a mutual admiration society—I'm secretly ogling him, too. He's taken off his shirt and is only wearing swim trunks, so I can finally see the lean, smooth muscles of his shoulders and chest and stomach. I want to memorize the landscape of him with my hands. I shiver and wrap my towel around my body. Olly misinterprets my shiver and steps close to me to add his towel to my shoulders. His skin smells like the ocean and something else, some indefinable thing that makes him Olly. I shock myself by wanting to touch my tongue to his chest, to taste the sun and salt on his skin. I drag my eyes away from his chest and up to his face. He avoids my eyes and wraps the towel tight around me so none of my skin is showing and then steps away from me. I get the feeling that he's holding himself in check.

I'm sure I don't want him to.

*

He looks over to the cliff where people, mostly teenagers, are leaping into the ocean. "Want to jump from a big rock?" he asks, eyes sparkling.

"I can't swim," I remind him.

"A little drowning never hurt anybody," says the boy who once warned me that the sea was merciless and unforgiving.

He grabs my hand and we run toward the cliff together. Up close the rocks look like hard black sponge. They're sharp against my feet and it takes me a while to find foot holes for each step, but eventually we make it to the top.

Olly's eager to jump. He doesn't even stop to admire the view.

"Together?" he asks, looking down at the sparkling water.

"Next time," I say.

He nods. "I'll go first. I won't let you drown." He jumps up and out and does a full somersault before arrowing into the water. A few seconds later he resurfaces and waves up to me. I wave back and then close my eyes to take stock of my situation, because jumping off a cliff seems like a pivotal moment where a little stock-taking should be done. Strangely, though, I find I don't really want to think too much. Like Olly, I just want to jump. I search out Olly's face in the water and find him waiting for me. Considering what the future may hold, jumping off this cliff doesn't seem so scary at all.

CLIFF DIVING: A GUIDE

OFF THE BEATEN PATH

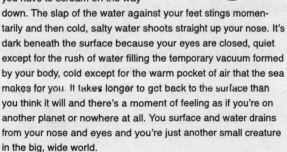

CLIFF DIVING

Here's what happens when you jump feetfirst and arms flailing off of a thirty-foot cliff into the Pacific Ocean. The fall is so thrilling that you have to scream on the way down. The slap of the water against your feet stings momentarily and then cold, salty water shoots straight up your nose. It's dark beneath the surface because your eyes are closed, quiet except for the rush of water filling the temporary vacuum formed by your body, cold except for the warm pocket of air that the sea makes for you. It takes longer to get back to the surface than you think it will and there's a moment of feeling as if you're on another planet or nowhere at all. You surface and water drains from your nose and eyes and you're just another small creature in the big, wide world.

ZACH

BACK AT THE hotel, Olly calls his friend Zach from our room phone. Half an hour later he's at our door.

Zach has dark umber skin and enormous dreadlocks and a smile that's almost too big for his face. He immediately begins playing air guitar and singing a song that I don't know. Olly grins from ear to ear. Zach thrashes his head dramatically while he "plays" and his hair keeps time with the "music."

"Zach!" Olly says, and pulls him into a hug. They slap each other's backs loudly.

"It's Zachariah now."

"Since when?" asks Olly.

"Since I decided to become a rock god. It's Zachariah like—"

"Messiah," I pipe in, getting his joke.

"Exactly! Your girlfriend is smarter than you are."

I blush and look over to see Olly blushing, too.

"Well that was cute," Zach says, laughing and strumming air-guitar strings. His laugh reminds me of Carla's—unselfconscious, a little too loud, and full of mirth. In that moment I miss her desperately.

Olly turns to me. "Maddy, this is Zach."

"Zachariah."

"Dude, I'm not calling you that. *Zach*, this is Maddy."

Zach takes my hand and gives it a quick kiss. "Fantastic to meet you, Maddy. I've heard a lot about you, but I didn't think you were really real."

"That's OK," I say, examining my hand where he kissed it. "Some days I'm not."

He laughs too loudly again and I find myself laughing with him.

"Wonderful," Olly cuts in. "Let's move this along. There's a loco moco with Maddy's name on it."

A loco moco is a mountain of rice topped with a hamburger patty topped with gravy topped with two fried eggs. Zach's taken us to a mixed-plate restaurant for a late lunch. We sit at a table outside, the ocean just a few hundred feet in the distance.

"This place is the best," Zach says. "It's where all the locals eat."

"You tell your parents yet?" Olly asks him in between bites.

"About the rockstar thing or the gay thing?"

"Both."

"Nope."

"You'll feel better once it's out there."

"No doubt, but the difficulty level is a little high."

Zach looks over to me. "My parents only believe in three things: family, education, and hard work. By 'family' I mean one man, one woman, two children, and a dog. By 'education' I mean a four-year college, and by 'hard work' I mean nothing involving art. Or hopes. Or rockstar dreams."

He looks back to Olly now and his brown eyes are more

serious than before. "How am I gonna tell them that their first-born son wants to be the African-American Freddie Mercury?"

"They must suspect," I say. "The rockstar part at least. Your hair is four different shades of red."

"They think it's a phase."

"Maybe you could write them a song."

His laugh booms. "I like you," he says.

"I like you, too," I say back. "You could call the song 'This Apple Has Fallen Very, Very, Very Far from the Tree.'"

"I'm not even sure I'm an apple," Zach says, laughing.

"You guys are funny," Olly says, almost smiling, but obviously preoccupied. "Dude, let me borrow your phone," he says to Zach.

Zach hands it over and Olly immediately starts typing.

"What's going on with you? Dad still a bastard?"

"You thought that would change?" He doesn't look up from the phone.

"I guess not," says Zach, a shrug in his voice. How much does he know about Olly's family? His dad is so much worse than just a bastard.

"What about you, Madeline? What's wrong with your parents?"

"It's just me and my mom."

"Still. There must be something wrong with her."

My mom, my mom. I've barely given her any thought. She must be crippled with worry.

"Well, I think there's something wrong with everyone, don't you? But my mom's smart, and she's strong, and she always puts me first."

I know I've surprised them because neither one speaks.

Olly looks up from Zach's phone. "You have to tell her you're OK, Mad."

He hands me the phone and leaves for the restroom.

⊠ 🖃 ⊠ ⊠ ⊠ ⊠

From: Madeline F. Whittier
To: genericuser033@gmail.com
Subject: (no subject)

Do you have my daughter? Is she OK?

From: Madeline F. Whittier
To: genericuser033@gmail.com
Subject: (no subject)

I know she's with you. You don't understand how sick she is. Bring her home.

From: Madeline F. Whittier
To: genericuser033@gmail.com
Subject: (no subject)

Please tell me where you are. She could get severely ill at any minute.

From: Madeline F. Whittier
To: genericuser033@gmail.com
Subject: (no subject)

I know where you are and I'm on the next flight. I'll be there first thing in the morning. Please keep her safe.

I stop reading, cradle the phone against my chest, and close my eyes. I'm guilty and resentful and panicked all at once. Seeing all her worry and pain makes me want to go to her and reassure her that I'm OK. That part of me wants to let her keep me safe.

But another part of me, the newer part, isn't ready to give up the world I'm starting to know. I resent that she's logged into my private e-mails. I resent that now Olly and I will have even less time than I thought.

My eyes are closed for too long because Zach finally asks if I'm OK.

I open my eyes and take a sip of pineapple juice, nodding around the straw.

"No, really. Are you feeling OK? Olly told me—"

"He told you I'm sick."

"Yeah."

"I'm fine," I say, realizing that I really do mean it. I feel fine. I feel more than fine.

I look back down at the phone. I need to say something.

From: genericuser033
To: Madeline F. Whittier <madeline.whittier@gmail.com>
Subject: (no subject)

Please don't worry, Mom. And please don't come here. I'm really OK and it's my life too. I love you. I'll see you soon.

I hit send and hand the phone back to Zach. He pockets it and stares at me.

"So you really bought pills off the Internet?" he asks.

I'm still so shaken up from my mom's e-mails and worrying that Olly and I don't have enough time for each other that I'm not prepared to hear my lie coming out of his mouth. I do exactly what you're not supposed to do when lying to someone: I don't meet his eyes. I fidget and blush.

I open my mouth to explain, but no explanation comes.

He's already guessed the truth by the time I finally meet his eyes.

"Are you going to tell him?" I ask.

"No. I've been lying about myself for so long. I know what it's like."

Relief washes over me. "Thank you," I say.

He just nods.

"What would happen if you told your parents?" I ask.

His answer is immediate. "They'd try to make me choose. And I wouldn't choose them. This way, everybody wins."

He leans back in his chair and strums. "All apologies to the Rolling Stones, but my first album's going to be called *Between Rock and Roll and a Hard Place*. What do you think?"

I laugh. "That's terrible."

He grows serious again. "Maybe growing up means disappointing the people we love."

It's not a question and, anyway, I don't have an answer.

I turn my head and watch Olly as he walks back toward us.

"Doing OK?" he asks before kissing my forehead and then my nose and then my lips.

I decide not to bring up my mom's impending visit. We'll just make the most of the time we have.

"I've never felt better in my life," I say. I'm grateful at least that I don't have to lie about this.

THE MURPHY BED

IT'S LATE AFTERNOON by the time we get back to the hotel. Olly flicks on all the lights and the ceiling fan and then does a diving somersault onto the bed.

He lies on one side and then the other. "This side is mine," he says, meaning the left side, closer to the door. "I sleep on the left," he says. "So you know. For future reference." He sits up and presses down on the mattress with his palms. "You know what I said before about Murphy beds being the height of comfort? I'm going to take that back."

"Are you nervous?" I blurt out. I turn on the lamp on the right side of the bed.

"No," he says, too quickly. He rolls over, drops off the side of the bed to the floor, and stays there.

I sit down at the edge of my side and bounce an experimental bounce. The mattress squeaks at me.

"Why do you sleep on the left when you sleep alone?" I ask. I move onto the bed and lie down. He's right. It's breathtakingly uncomfortable.

"Maybe it's anticipation," he says.

"Of what?"

He doesn't answer, so I roll over to peer down at him. He's lying on his back, one arm flung across his eyes.

"Company," he says.

I retract my head, blushing. "You're kind of a hopeless romantic," I say.

"Sure. Sure."

We slip into quiet. Above us the fan whirs softly, coaxing warm air around the room. Through the doors I hear the ding of the elevators and the low murmur of passing voices.

A few days ago just a single day outside seemed like it would be enough, but now that I've had one, I want more. I'm not sure if forever would do.

"Yes," Olly says after a while. "I'm nervous."

"Why?"

He takes a breath that I don't hear him release. "I've never felt about anybody the way I feel about you." He doesn't say it quietly. If anything, he says it too loudly and all in a rush, as if the words have been wanting to tumble out for a long time.

I sit up on my elbows, lie back down, sit up again. Are we talking about love?

"I've never felt this way either," I whisper.

"But it's different for you." There's frustration in his voice.

"Why? How?"

"It's your first time for everything, Maddy, but it's not for me."

I don't understand. Just because it's the first time doesn't make it less real, does it? Even the universe has a beginning.

He's silent. The more I think about what he's saying, the more upset I get. But then I realize that he's not trying to dismiss or belittle my feelings. He's just scared. Given my lack of choices, what if I've just chosen him by default?

He takes a breath. "In my head I know I've been in love before, but it doesn't feel like it. Being in love with you is better than the first time. It feels like the first time and the last time and the only time all at once."

"Olly," I say, "I promise you that I know my own heart. It's one of the few things that's not completely new to me."

He climbs back into bed and throws an arm out. I curl into him, put my head into the Maddy-shaped nook of space between his neck and shoulder.

"I love you, Maddy."

"I love you, Olly. I loved you before I knew you."

We drift off to sleep curled around each other, neither of us talking, just letting the world make some noise for us for a while because all the other words don't matter right now.

ALL THE WORDS

I COME AWAKE slowly, languidly, until I realize what we've done. I glance at the clock. We've been asleep for over an hour. We barely have any time left and we've spent some of it sleeping. I glance at the clock again. Ten minutes to shower and another ten to find the perfect spot on the beach to watch our first and last day together come to an end.

I shake Olly awake and rush to get dressed. In the bathroom, I slip into my one-size-fits-all dress. One size can fit all because the skirt flares out and the top is ribbed elastic that can stretch to accommodate most anyone. Forgoing my scrunchie, I let my hair have its way, and it falls curly and full around my shoulders and down my back. In the mirror my skin glows a warm brown and my eyes glitter.

I am the picture of health.

Olly's seated on the top rung of the railing on the lanai. His position looks precarious, even though he's holding on to the railing with both hands. I remind myself he has plenty of control over his body.

He smiles, more than smiles, when he sees me. He's Olly and not-Olly again, eyes sharp and tracking my approach. I'm aware of every single sparking nerve in my body. How does he do that with just a look? Do I have the same effect on him? I stop at the sliding glass doors and look him over. He's wearing a close-fitting black T-shirt, black shorts, and black sandals. The angel of death on vacation.

"Come here," he says, and I nestle into the V of his legs. He goes still and his grip on the rail tightens. I inhale the fresh scent of him and look up. His eyes are a clear, summer-blue lake that I can't see the bottom of. I touch my lips to his. He hops down from the railing, pushing me back against a table. Before I know it, I'm flush against him and he's kissing me with a groan. I open for him and we kiss until I can't breathe, until my next breath is one of his. My hands are on his shoulders, on the back of his neck, in his hair. My hands don't know where to stop. I am electrified. I want everything, and all at once. He breaks our kiss and we stand there, drawing ragged breaths, foreheads and noses touching, his hands gripping too hard on my hips, my hands flat against his chest.

"Maddy." His eyes are a question and I say yes. Because it was always going to be yes.

"What about the sunset?" he asks.

I shake my head. "There'll be another one tomorrow."

He looks relieved, and I can't help but smile. He walks me backward through the lanai doors until the backs of my knees are pressed into the bed.

I sit. And then stand right back up. It was easier jumping from Black Rock than doing this.

"Maddy, we don't have to."

"No. I want to. This is what I want."

He nods and then squeezes his eyes shut, remembering something. "I have to go buy—"

I shake my head. "I have some."

"You have some what?" he asks, not catching on.

"Condoms, Olly. I have some."

"You have some."

"Yes," I say, my entire body blushing.

"When?"

"At the souvenir shop. Fourteen ninety-nine. That place has everything."

He looks at me as if I were a small miracle, but then his smile turns into something more. Then I'm on my back, and his hand is tugging at my dress.

"Off. Off," he says.

I scramble to my knees and pull it off over my head. I shiver in the warm air.

"You have freckles here, too," he says, sliding his hand across the tops of my breasts.

I look down to confirm and we both laugh.

He puts his hand on my bare waist. "You're all the good things wrapped into one good thing."

"Um, you too," I say, inarticulate. All the words in my head have been replaced with one—*Olly*.

He pulls his T-shirt off over his head and my body takes over my brain. I run my fingertips over the smooth hard muscles of his chest, dip them into the valleys between them. My lips follow the same path, tasting, caressing. He lies back and keeps himself still, letting me explore, and I kiss my way across the landscape of him down to his toes and back up again. The urge to bite him is irresistible and I don't resist it. The bite pushes him over the edge and he takes charge. My body burns where he doesn't touch, and burns where he does.

We gather each other up. We are lips and arms and legs and bodies entangled. He raises himself above me and we are wordless, and then we are joined and moving silently. We are joined and I know all of the secrets of the universe.

MADELINE'S DICTIONARY

in•fi•nite (ˈinfənit) *adj.* **1.** The state
of not knowing where one body
ends and another begins: *Our joy is
infinite.* [2015, *Whittier*]

THE OBSERVABLE WORLD

ACCORDING TO THE Big Bang theory, the universe came into being in one single moment—a cosmic cataclysm that gave birth to black holes, brown dwarfs, matter and dark matter, energy and dark energy. It gave birth to galaxies and stars and moons and suns and planets and oceans. It's a hard concept to hold on to—the idea that there was a time before us. A time before time.

In the beginning there was nothing. And then there was everything.

THIS TIME

OLLY SMILES. HE will not stop smiling. He gives me every variation of smile that there is and I have to kiss his smiling lips. One kiss leads to ten until our kissing is interrupted by the sound of Olly's stomach growling.

I break our kiss. "I guess we should eat something."

"Besides you?" He kisses my bottom lip and then bites it gently. "You are delicious, but inedible."

I sit up, holding the blanket to my chest. I'm not quite ready to be naked again despite our intimacy. Unlike me, Olly's not feeling at all shy. He's out of bed in a single movement and moves about the room completely naked. I lean back against the headboard and simply watch him move, all grace and light. No dark angel of death now.

Everything's different and the same. I'm still Maddy. Olly's still Olly. But we're both more somehow. I know him in a new way. And I feel known, too.

The restaurant sits right on the beach and our table faces the ocean. It's late—9 P.M.—so we can't really see the blue of the water, just the whitecaps of the waves as they crash against the beach. We hear it just beneath the music and chatter all around us.

"Think they have humuhumu on the menumenu?" Olly teases. He jokes that he wants to eat all the fish that we saw while snorkeling.

"I'm going to guess that they don't serve the state fish," I say.

We're both starving from all the activity of the day, so we order every appetizer on the menu: poke (tuna marinated in soy sauce), crab cakes, coconut shrimp, lobster pot stickers, and Kalua pork. We don't stop touching for the entire meal. We touch in between bites of food and sips of pineapple juice. He touches the side of my neck, my cheek, my lips. I touch his fingers, his forearms, his chest. Now that we've touched so intimately, we can't stop.

We move the chairs so that we're sitting right next to each other. He holds my hand in his lap or I hold his in mine. We look at each other and laugh for no reason. Or, not for no reason, but because the world just then seems extraordinary. For us to have met, to have fallen in love, to get to be together is beyond anything either of us had ever thought possible.

Olly orders us a second helping of lobster pot stickers. "You make me very hungry," he croons, eyebrows waggling. He touches my cheek and I blush into his hands. We eat this plate more slowly. It's our last. Maybe if we just sit here, if we don't acknowledge that time is passing, then this too-perfect day won't have to end.

As we leave, the waitress tells us to come back and visit again soon, and Olly promises that we will.

We head away from the lights of the restaurant and toward the darkened beach. Above, the clouds have hidden the moon. We slip off our sandals, walk close to the water's edge, and sink our toes into the cooling sand. Nighttime waves crash mightier and louder than daytime ones. The farther we walk, the fewer people we see, until it begins to feel as though we've left civilization behind. Olly steers us to dry sand and we find a place to sit.

He takes my hand and kisses the palm. "My dad apologized to us after he hit her the first time." He pushes the sentence out on a single breath. It takes me a second to realize what he's talking about.

"He was crying."

The night is so dark that I feel rather than see him shake his head.

"They sat us down together and he said he was sorry. He said it would never happen again. I remember Kara was so angry she wouldn't even look at him. She knew he was a liar, but I believed him. My mom did, too. She told us to forget all about it. She said, 'Your father has been through a lot.' She said that she forgave him and that we should, too."

He gives me my hand back. "He didn't hit her again for another year. He drank too much. He yelled at her. He yelled at all of us. But he didn't hit her again for a long time."

I hold my breath for a moment and ask the question I've been wanting to ask. "Why doesn't she leave him?"

He snorts and his tone turns hard. "Don't think I haven't asked her." He lies back in the sand, links his hands behind his head. "I think that if he hit her more often, she would leave him. If he were just a little more of a bastard maybe we could finally go. But he's always sorry, and she always believes him."

I put my hand on his stomach, needing the contact. I think maybe he needs it, too, but then he sits up, pulls his knees into his chest, and rests his elbows on them. His body forms a cage that I can't get into.

"What does she say when you ask her?"

"Nothing. She won't talk about it anymore. She used to say that we'd understand when we're older and in our own relationships."

I'm surprised by the anger in his voice. I never guessed that he was angry at his mother. His father, yes, but not her.

He snorts again. "She says love makes people crazy."

"Do you believe that?"

"Yes. No. Maybe."

"You're not supposed to use all the answers," I say.

He smiles in the dark. "Yes, I believe it."

"Why?"

"I'm all the way here in Hawaii with you. It's not easy for me to leave them alone with him."

I tamp down my guilt before it can rise.

"Do *you* believe it?" he asks.

"Yes. Definitely."

"Why?"

"I'm all the way here in Hawaii with you," I say, repeating his words. "I never would've left my house if it weren't for you."

"So," he says. He lowers his legs and takes my hand. "What do we do now?"

I don't know the answer to this question. The only thing I know for sure is that this—being here with Olly, being able to love him and be loved by him—is everything.

"You should leave them," I say. "It's not safe for you there." I say it because he doesn't know it. He's trapped by the same memory of love, of better times, that his mother is, and it isn't enough.

I rest my head on his shoulder and we watch the near-dark ocean together. We watch the way the water pulls back and turns over and beats against the sand, trying to wear the earth away. And even though it doesn't succeed, it pulls back and pounds the shore again and again, as if there were no last time and there is no next time and this time is the time that counts.

SPIRAL

I dream that I've run away from home taking the boy I love with me. I dream that I saw the ocean and it was endless and that I've run away from home taking the boy that loves me and that I dream that I saw the ocean and it was endless and that I could not find the end of it. I dream that I saw the ocean and it was endless and that I could not find the end of it. I dream that I fall asleep in an unquiet room with the boy I love with me. I dream that I fall asleep in an unquiet room and that I dream about the life I'm leaving

THE END

SOMEONE HAS PUT me in a hot oven and locked the door.

Someone has doused me in kerosene and lit a match.

I come awake slowly with my body on fire, consumed in flames. The sheets are cold and damp. I'm drowning in sweat.

What's happening to me? It takes a moment before I realize that there are many, many things wrong.

I'm shivering. I'm more than shivering. I'm shaking uncontrollably and my head *hurts*. My brain is being squeezed in a vise. Pain radiates out and crashes into the nerves behind my eyes.

My body is a fresh bruise. Even my skin hurts.

At first I think I must be dreaming, but my dreams are never this lucid. I try to sit up, to pull the blankets closer, but I can't. Olly's still asleep and lying on top of them.

I try again to sit up, but pain buries itself deep in my bones.

The vise around my brain tightens and now there's an ice pick stabbing indiscriminately at the soft flesh.

I try to cry out but my throat is raw, as if I'd been screaming for days and days.

I'm sick.

I'm more than sick. I'm dying.

Oh, God. Olly.

This is going to break his heart.

He awakes as soon as I think it. "Mad?" he asks into the dark.

He turns on the bedside lamp and my eyes burn. I squeeze them shut and try to turn away. I don't want him to see me like this, but it's too late. I watch his face go from confusion, to recognition, to disbelief. Then terror.

"I'm sorry," I say, or try to say, but I don't think the words make it past my lips.

He touches my face, my neck, my forehead.

"Jesus," he says, over and over again. "Jesus."

He pulls the blanket off and I'm colder than I'd ever thought possible.

"Jesus, Maddy, you're burning up."

"Cold," I croak, and he looks even more terrified.

He covers me and cradles my head, kisses my wet brow, lips.

"You're fine," he says. "You're going to be fine."

I'm not, but it's nice of him to say so. My body pulses with pain and my throat feels like it's swelling shut. I can't get enough air.

"I need an ambulance," I hear him say.

I roll my head around. When did he get to that side of the room? Where are we? He's on the phone. He's talking about someone. Someone sick. Someone *is* sick. Dying. Emergency. Pills not working.

He's talking about me.

He's crying. Don't cry. Kara will be fine. Your mom will be fine. You will be fine.

The bed sinks. I'm in quicksand. Someone's trying to pull

235

me out. His hands are hot. Why are they so hot?

Something glows in his other hand. It's his cell phone. He's saying something, but the words won't come clear. Something. Mom. *Your* mom.

Yes. Mom. I need my mom. She's already on her way. I hope she's close.

I close my eyes and squeeze his fingers.

I'm out of time.

My.
Heart.
Stops.

And starts again.

RELEASED, PART ONE

Maui Memorial Discharge Form

Medical Record #:   Patient Name: *Whittier, Madeline*   Location: *Maui Memorial*   (Revised 12-1-10)

Admit Date: Discharge Date: Physician: *Francis, Melissa*

Demographic	Age: _18_ years or Date of Birth: _5_ / _2_ / _1997_ Gender: ☐Male ☒Female Race: ☐white ☐black/african american ☐asian ☐hispanic ☐native american ☒multiracial ☐other ☐don't know
Cardiac Diagnosis	☐Chest pain, r/o MI ☐Confirmed AMI ☐CHF, Pulmonary edema ☐Coronary artery disease ☐Unstable Angina ☐Syncope ☐Cerebral vascular disease ☐Peripheral vascular disease ☒Other
Procedures	☐None ☐Cardiac catheterization ☐PTCA ☐PTCA with stent ☐PCI ☒Echocardiogram ☐RVG ☐ETT ☐Nuclear ETT ☐Coronary artery bypass graft ☐Cardiac valve ☐MUGA ☐Exercise Echo ☐Other
What does the patient's past history include?	☐Previous MI ☐Angina ☐Heart failure ☐Hypertension ☐Diabetes ☐Renal insufficiency ☐Smoker (within the past year) ☐No regular exercise (<30min. 3x/wk) ☐ PVD ☐ Stroke ☐COPD ☐Atrial fibrillation ☒Unknown ☐None of the above
Discharge Status	☐01 - Discharge home ☐02 - Discharge to another hospital ☐03 - Discharge to skilled nursing facility (SNF) ☐04 - Discharge to intermediate care facility (ICF) ☐06 - Discharge home health care organization	☒07 - Left against advice ☐10 - Transfer to chronic or rehabilitation hospital ☐11 - Discharge to mental health setting ☐12 - Discharge other ☐20 – Expired

RESURRECTED

I DON'T REMEMBER much, just a jumbled mix of images. The ambulance. Being stabbed in the leg once. Then twice. Adrenaline shots to restart my heart. Sirens wailing from far away, and then much too close. A TV flickering blue and white high in a corner of the room. Machines beeping and blinking all day and all night keeping vigil. Women and men in white uniforms. Stethoscopes and needles and antiseptics.

Then that smell of jet fuel, that smell that welcomed me before, and leis and the scratchy blanket wrapped twice around me, and why does the window seat matter when the shades are drawn closed?

I remember my mother's face and how her tears could make a sea.

I remember Olly's blue eyes gone black. I closed mine against the sorrow and relief and love I saw there.

I'm on my way home. I'll remain trapped there forever.

I'm alive and don't want to be.

READMITTED

MY MOM HAS transformed my bedroom into a hospital ward. I'm propped up by pillows in my bed and attached to an IV. I'm surrounded by monitoring equipment. I eat nothing but Jell-O.

Each time I awake, she's by my side. She touches my forehead and speaks to me. Sometimes I try to focus, to understand what she's saying, but the sound is just out of my reach.

I wake again sometime (hours? days?) later to find her standing over me, frowning at her clipboard. I close my eyes and take inventory of my body. Nothing hurts or, more accurately, nothing hurts too badly. I check in on my head, my throat, my legs. They're all fine. I open my eyes again to find her about to put me back to sleep.

"No!" I sit up much too quickly. I'm dizzy and nauseous at once. I mean to say *I'm OK,* but no sound comes out.

I clear my throat and try again. "Please don't make me sleep anymore." I at least need to be awake if I'm going to be alive. "Am I OK?" I ask.

"You're OK. You're going to be OK," she says. Her voice trembles until it breaks.

I pull myself to seated and look at her. Her skin is pale, almost translucent, and it's stretched too tight across her face. A painful-looking blue vein stretches down from her hairline to her eyelid. I can see other blue veins just under the skin of her forearms and wrists. She has the frightened, disbelieving eyes of someone who witnessed something horrible and is waiting for more horrors to come.

"How could you do this to yourself? You could've died," she whispers

She steps closer, hugs a clipboard to her chest. "How could you do this to me? After everything?"

I want to say something. I open my mouth to say it, but nothing comes out.

My guilt is an ocean for me to drown in.

I remain in bed after she leaves. I don't get up to stretch my body. I turn my face away from the window. What do I regret? That I went outside in the first place. That I saw and fell in love with the world. That I fell in love with Olly. How can I live the rest of my life in this bubble now that I know all that I'm missing?

I close my eyes and try to sleep. But the sight of my mom's face earlier, all the desperate love in her eyes, won't leave me. I decide then that love is a terrible, terrible thing. Loving someone as fiercely as my mom loves me must be like wearing your heart outside of your body with no skin, no bones, no nothing to protect it.

Love is a terrible thing and its loss is even worse.

Love is a terrible thing and I want nothing to do with it.

RELEASED, PART TWO

Wednesday, 6:56 P.M.

Olly: jesus, where have you been?

Olly: are you ok?

Madeline: Yes.

Olly: what does your mom say?

Olly: are you going to be ok?

Madeline: I'm OK, Olly.

Olly: i tried to visit you but your mom wouldn't let me

Madeline: She's protecting me.

Olly: i know

Madeline: Thanks for saving my life.

Madeline: I'm sorry I put you through all that.

Olly: you don't have to thank me

Madeline: Thank you anyway.

Olly: are you sure you're OK?

Madeline: Please don't ask me that anymore.

Olly: sorry

Madeline: Don't be.

Later, 9:33 P.M.

Olly: it's nice being able to IM you again

Olly: you were a terrible mime

Olly: say something

Olly: I know you're disappointed Mad but at least you're alive

Olly: we'll talk to your mom once you're better again. maybe i can visit

Olly: I know it's not everything Mad but it's better than nothing

Later, 12:05 A.M.

Madeline: It's not better than nothing. It's absolutely worse than nothing.

Olly: what?

Madeline: Do you think we can go back to the way it was before?

Madeline: You want to go back to decontamination, and short visits, and no touching and no kissing and no future?

Madeline: You're saying that's enough for you?

Olly: it's better than nothing

Madeline: No it's not. Stop saying that.

Later, 2:33 A.M.

Olly: what about the pills?

Madeline: What about them?

Olly: they worked for a couple of days. maybe they'll get them right eventually

Olly: maddy?

Madeline: There were no pills.

Olly: what do you mean?

Madeline: There were never any pills. I told you that so that you would go with me.

Olly: you lied to me?

Olly: but you could've died and it would've been my fault

Madeline: I'm not your responsibility.

Later, 3:42 A.M.

Madeline: I wanted everything, Olly. I wanted you and the whole wide world. I wanted everything.

Madeline: I can't do this anymore.

Olly: can't do what?

Madeline: No more IM. No more e-mail. It's too hard. I can't go back. My mom was right. Life was better before.

Olly: better for who?

Olly: don't do this Maddy

Olly: my life is better with you in it

Madeline: but mine isn't

<Madeline has logged out>

LIFE IS SHORT™

SPOILER REVIEWS BY MADELINE

INVISIBLE MAN BY RALPH ELLISON

Spoiler alert: You don't exist if no one can see you.

GEOGRAPHY

I'M IN AN endless field filled with red poppies. The poppies reach waist high on single green stalks and are so red they seem to bleed color. In the distance I see one Olly, and then two, and then multiple Ollys marching toward me. They're wearing gas masks and holding handcuffs and crushing the poppies under black-booted feet as they march toward me, silent and determined.

The dream doesn't leave me. I drift through the day awake but dreaming, trying not to think of Olly. I try not to think of seeing him for the first time. How he seemed like he was from another planet. I try not to think about Bundt cakes and headstands and kisses and velvet sand. How second and third and fourth kisses are just as amazing as first ones. I try not to think about him moving inside me and us moving together. I try not to think of him because if I do, I'll have to think about how connected to him and the world I was just a few days go.

I'll have to think of all the hope I had. Of how I fooled myself into thinking that I was a miracle. Of how the world I wanted to be a part of so badly didn't want me back.

I have to let Olly go. I've learned my lesson. Love *can* kill you and I'd rather be alive than out there living.

I once told Olly that I knew my own heart better than I knew anything else, and it's still true. I know the places in my heart, but the names have all changed.

MAP OF DESPAIR

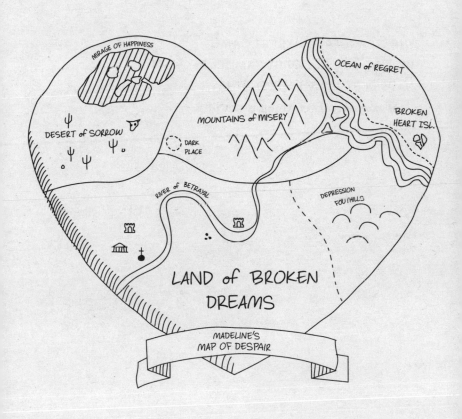

MIRAGE OF HAPPINESS

OCEAN OF REGRET

MOUNTAINS of MISERY

BROKEN
HEART ISL.

DESERT of SORROW

DARK
PLACE

RIVER of BETRAYAL

DEPRESSION
FOOTHILLS

LAND of BROKEN
DREAMS

MADELINE'S
MAP OF DESPAIR

LIFE IS SHORT™
SPOILER REVIEWS BY MADELINE

THE STRANGER BY ALBERT CAMUS

WAITING FOR GODOT BY SAMUEL BECKETT

NAUSEA BY JEAN-PAUL SARTRE

    Spoiler alert: Everything is nothing.

SELECT ALL, DELETE

| | | | | | 1-25 of 2,814 | ◄ | ► | ⚙ |

COMPOSE

INBOX (64)
SENT MAIL
DRAFTS
TRASH
MORE ▼

☑	genericuser033	limerick #1	6:14am
☑	genericuser033	please maddy	6:05am
☑	genericuser033	ill just monologue here	5:59am
☑	genericuser033	im not going away	5:50am
☑	genericuser033	for when you emerge again someday	5:41am
☑	genericuser033	🗄 ARCHIVE	5:32am
☑	genericuser033	📁 MOVE	
☑	genericuser033	🗑 DELETE	5:22am
☑	genericuser033	mom is cooking again (exclusive pics)	5:19am
☑	genericuser033	the meaning of maddy pt. the fourth	5:08am
☑	genericuser033	misery update	5:01am
☑	genericuser033	me again	

PRETENDING

I'M STRONGER WITH each passing day. Nothing hurts except my heart, but I'm trying not to use it. I keep the blinds closed. I read my books. Existential or nihilist ones. I have no patience for books that pretend life has meaning. I have no patience for happy endings.

I don't think about Olly. He sends me e-mails that I trash without reading.

After two weeks I'm strong enough to resume some classes. Another two weeks and I'm able to resume all of them.

I don't think about Olly. I trash still more of his e-mails.

My mom is still trying to fix me. She hovers. And worries and fusses and administers. Now that I'm stronger she coaxes me back into our mother-daughter nights. Like Olly, she wants our lives to go back to the way they were before. I don't enjoy our nights together—I don't really enjoy anything—but I do it for her. She's lost even more weight. I'm alarmed and don't know how to fix her, so I play Fonetik Skrabbl and Honor Pictionary and watch movies and pretend.

Olly's e-mails stop.

"I've asked Carla to come back," she says one night after dinner.

"I thought you didn't trust her anymore."

"But I trust *you*. You learned your lesson the hard way. Some things you just have to experience for yourself."

REUNION

THE NEXT DAY, Carla bustles in. Her bustle is even *bustlier* than normal, and she pretends no time has passed at all.

She gathers me up immediately. "I'm sorry," she says. "It's all my fault."

I hold myself stiff against her, not wanting to dissolve. If I cry, everything will be real. I really will have to live this life. I really will never see Olly again.

I try to hold out but I can't. She's the soft pillow you're supposed to cry into. Once I start, I don't stop for an hour. She's soaked and I don't have any tears left. Can you reach the end of tears? I wonder.

I answer my own question by crying some more.

"How's your mama?" she asks when I finally stop.

"She doesn't hate me."

"Mamas don't know how to hate their babies. They love them too much."

"But she should. I'm a terrible daughter. I did a terrible thing."

More tears leak out, but Carla wipes them away with the side of her hand.

"And your Olly?"

I shake my head at her. I would tell Carla anything, but not this. My heart is too bruised and I want to keep the pain as a reminder. I don't want sunlight on it. I don't want it to heal. Because if it does, I might be tempted to use it again.

We settle back into our normal routine. Each day is like the one before and not much different from the next. *Madam, I'm Adam.* I'm working on a model of a library with an Escher-like interior of staircases that end midstep and go nowhere. From Outside, I hear a rumble and then a beeping. This time I immediately know what it is.

At first I don't go to the window. But Carla does and narrates what she sees. It's a moving van—Two Brothers Moving. The brothers get out of the van and unload dollies and empty boxes and packing tape. They talk to Olly's mom. Kara and Olly are there. There's no dad in sight, she says.

My curiosity gets the better of me, and I'm at the window peering out the other side of the curtain. Carla's right. Olly's dad is nowhere to be found. Olly and Kara and his mom seem frantic. They rush in and out of the house, leaving packed boxes or bulging plastic garbage bags on the porch for the movers to load onto the truck. No one's talking. I can tell his mom is nervous even from here. Every few minutes Olly stops and pulls her into a hug. She clings to him and he pats her back. Kara doesn't join them. She smokes openly now, ashing her cigarette directly onto the porch.

I'm trying not to focus on Olly, but it's impossible. My heart doesn't care at all what my brain thinks. I see the exact moment that he feels my eyes on him. He stops what he's doing and turns. Our eyes meet. It's different than that first time. The first time was all about possibility. Even then, some part of me knew that I would love him.

This time is about certainty. I already know that I love him, and I know now that I won't stop.

He raises his hand to wave. I let go of the curtain, turn away, and press my back against the wall, breathing hard.

I wish I could undo the last few months of knowing him. I would stay in my room. I would hear the truck beeping next door and I would remain on my white couch in my white room reading my brand-new books. I would remember my past and then I would remember not to repeat it.

NEIGHBORHOOD WATCH #3

HIS DAD'S SCHEDULE
    9:00 AM – Leaves for work.
    8:30 PM – Sways unsteadily up the porch and into the
               house. Already drunk?
    9:00 PM – Arrives back on porch, drink in hand.
    10:15 PM – Passes out in blue chair.
    Sometime later: Stumbles into house.

HIS MOM'S SCHEDULE
    Unknown

KARA'S SCHEDULE
    Unknown

OLLY'S SCHEDULE
    Unknown

FIVE SYLLABLES

A MONTH LATER, just after Christmas, his dad moves away, too. Through my window I watch him carry just a few boxes to a U-Haul truck. I hope against hope that he's not going to wherever Olly and Kara and their mom are.

For days after I stare at the house, wondering how it can still manage to look the same, to seem so solid and house-like when there's no one around to make it a home.

I wait another couple of days before finally reading the e-mails that Olly has sent. They're still in the trash folder, as I knew they would be.

From: genericuser033
To: Madeline F. Whittier<madeline.whittier@gmail.com>
Subject: limerick #1
Sent: October 16, 6:14 AM

once was a girl named madeline
speared my heart through with a javelin
said i as i died
(just as an aside)
are there more words that rhyme with madeline?

From: genericuser033
To: Madeline F. Whittier<madeline.whittier@gmail.com>
Subject: limerick #2
Sent: October 17, 8:03 PM

once lived a girl in a bubble
who i suspected was nothing but trouble
still i gave her my heart
but she blew it apart
and left me with nothing but rubble

I laugh until I cry. He must've been really upset with me to send me limericks instead of haiku.

His other e-mails are less poetic. He tells me about trying to convince his mom to get some help and about trying to save Kara from herself. He's not sure which conversation with his mom finally convinced her. It could've been because he told her he couldn't be part of the family anymore if she stayed. Sometimes you have to leave the people who love you the most, he said. Or, he says, it could've been when he finally told her about me and about how sick I am and how I was willing to do anything just to live. He says that she thinks I'm brave.

HIS LAST LETTER IS HAIKU

From: genericuser033

To: Madeline F. Whittier<madeline.whittier@gmail.com>

Subject: haiku #1

Sent: October 31, 9:07 PM

five syllables here
and now here are seven more
i love you maddy

HERE AND NOW

OLLY'S MATH SAYS you can't predict the future. It turns out that you can't predict the past either. Time moves in both directions—forward and backward—and what happens here and now changes them both.

FOR MY EYES ONLY

From: Dr. Melissa Francis
To: madeline.whittier@gmail.com
Subject: Test Results - FOR YOUR EYES ONLY
Sent: December 29, 8:03 AM

Ms. Whittier,

You probably don't remember me. My name is Dr. Melissa Francis. You were under my care at Maui Memorial in Hawaii for a few hours two months ago.

I felt it was important to contact you directly. You need to know that I've studied your case very closely. I don't believe you have, or have ever had, SCID.

I know this must be a shock. I've attached quite a few test results here and I recommend that you get a second (and a third) opinion.

I believe that you should get another physician besides your mother to verify my findings. Physicians should never practice on their families.

It is my medical opinion that in Hawaii you had an episode of myocarditis triggered by a viral infection. I believe that your immune system is especially fragile given what I could surmise about the nature of your upbringing.

Please feel free to contact me with any questions you may have. Good luck.

Best regards,
Dr. Melissa Francis

PROTECTION

I READ THE e-mail six times before the letters form words and the words form sentences that I can understand, but, even then, the meaning of all the words taken together eludes me. I move on to the attachment showing lab test results. All my numbers are adamantly average—not too high, not too low.

Of course there's some mistake. *Of course* this is not right. Dr. Francis has confused my chart with someone else's. There's another Madeline Whittier. She's an inexperienced doctor. The world is casually cruel.

I believe all these things to be true, but still. I print the e-mail, lab test results and all. I'm not moving in slow motion. Time does not speed up or slow down.

The words on the printout are not any different than the ones on the screen, but they feel heavier, more weighty. But they can't be true. There's no possibility of them being true.

I spend an hour googling each test, trying to understand what they all mean. Of course the Internet can't tell me if these results are correct, can't tell me if I'm a perfectly average teenage girl of perfectly average health.

And I know. I *know* it's a mistake. Still, my feet are taking me down the stairs and through the dining room to my mother's home office. She's not there, and not in the den. I head to her bedroom and knock lightly, hands shaking. She doesn't answer. I hear running water. She's probably in her bathroom getting ready for bed. I knock again loudly.

"Mom," I call out as I turn the handle.

She's just leaving the bathroom, turning out the light when I walk in.

Her still-gaunt face breaks into a wide smile when she sees me. Her cheekbones are sharp and more prominent in her narrower face. The dark circles that I put under her eyes seem to have become permanent. She's not wearing any makeup and her hair hangs loosely around her shoulders. Black silk pajamas hang from her thin frame.

"Hi, sweetheart," she says. "Did you come for a slumber party?" Her face is so hopeful that I want to say yes.

I step farther into the room, shaking the pages. "It's from a doctor in Maui." I look for the name again even though I know it. "Dr. Melissa Francis. Did you meet her?"

If I hadn't been watching her so closely I might not have noticed it, but she freezes. "I met a lot of doctors in Maui, Madeline." Her voice is tight.

"Mom, I'm sorry—"

She holds up a hand telling me to stop. "What is it, Madeline?"

I take another step. "This letter. She, Dr. Francis, thinks I'm not sick."

She stares at me as if I haven't spoken. She doesn't speak for so long that I begin to question if I have spoken after all.

"What are you talking about?"

"She says she doesn't think I have SCID. She doesn't think I've ever had it."

She lowers herself to the edge of the bed. "Oh, no. Is this why you came to see me?"

Her voice is soft, pitying. "She got your hopes up, didn't she?"

She gestures for me to come and sit beside her. She takes the letter from my hands and wraps her arms around me. "I'm sorry, but it's not true," she says.

I sag into her arms. She's right. I had gotten my hopes up. Her arms feel so good around me. I feel warm and protected and safe.

She strokes my hair. "I'm sorry you had to see this. It's so irresponsible."

"It's OK," I say against her shoulder. "I knew it was a mistake. I didn't get my hopes up."

She pulls away to look into my eyes. "Of course it's a mistake."

Her eyes fill with tears and she pulls me back into her arms. "SCID is so rare and so complicated, honey. Not everyone understands it. There are just so many versions and every person reacts a little differently."

She pulls away again and meets my eyes to make sure I'm listening and understanding. Her speech slows down and her tone turns sympathetic—her doctor's voice. "You saw that for yourself, didn't you? You were fine for a little while and then you were almost dead in an emergency room. Immune systems are complicated."

She frowns down at the pages in her hand. "And this Dr. Francis doesn't know your full medical history. She's just seeing a tiny fraction of it. She hasn't been with you this whole time."

Her frown deepens. This mistake is upsetting her more than it did me.

"Mom, it's OK," I say. "I didn't really believe it anyway."

I don't think she hears me. "I had to protect you," she says.

"I know, Mom." I don't really want to talk about this anymore. I move back into her arms.

"I had to protect you," she says into my hair.

And it's that last "I had to protect you" that makes a part of me go quiet.

There's an uncertainty to her voice that I don't expect and can't account for.

I try to pull away, to see her face, but she holds on tight.

"Mom," I say, pulling harder.

She lets me go, caresses my face with her free hand.

I frown at her. "Can I have those?" I ask, meaning the papers in her hand.

She looks down and seems confused about how they got there. "You don't need these," she says, but gives them back to me anyway. "Want to have a slumber party?" she asks again, patting the bed. "I'll feel better if you stay with me."

But I'm not sure I will.

MADELINE'S DICTIONARY

sus•pi•cion (sə'spiSHən) *n. pl.* **-s**
1. The truth you don't believe, can't believe, won't believe: *Her suspicion of her mother keeps her awake all night.* | *She had a burgeoning suspicion that the world was laughing at her.* [2015, *Whittier*]

IDENTITY

CARLA'S BARELY IN the door before I'm on her with the letter. She reads it and her eyes widen with each sentence.

She grips my forearm. "Where did you get this?"

"Keep reading," I say. The charts and measurements will mean more to her than they did to me.

I watch her face and try to understand what is happening in my world. I'd expected her to dismiss the letter out of hand just as Mom did, but her reaction is . . . different.

"Have you shown this to your mother?"

I nod, mute.

"What did she say?"

"That it was a mistake." I'm whispering, hiding from the sound of my own voice.

She searches my face for a long time. "We need to find out," she says.

"Find out what?"

"If it's true or not."

"How could it be true? That would mean—"

"Shh, shh. We don't know anything yet."

We don't know anything? Of course we do. We know that I'm sick. That I'm not allowed to leave my house on pain of death. I've always known this. It is who I am.

"What's going on?" I demand. "What are you hiding from me?"

"No, no. I'm not hiding anything."

"What does this mean?"

She sighs, and it is long and deep and weary. "I swear I don't know anything. But sometimes I suspect."

"Suspect what?"

"Sometimes I think maybe your mama's not quite right. Maybe she never recovered from what happened to your papa and brother."

The oxygen in the room is replaced by something else, something thin and not-breathable. Time does slow down now and I get a kind of tunnel vision. The walls are much too close and Carla recedes away from me, a small figure at the end of a very long hallway. Tunnel vision gives way to vertigo. I'm unsteady on my feet and then nauseous.

I run to the bathroom and dry heave into the sink. Carla comes in as I'm splashing water on my face.

She puts her hand on my back and I sink under the weight of it. I'm insubstantial. I'm Olly's ghost girl again. I press my hands into the porcelain of the sink. I can't lift my eyes to the mirror because I won't recognize the girl looking back at me.

"I have to know for sure," I growl, using someone else's voice.

"Give me a day," she says, and tries to pull me into a hug, but I don't let her. I don't want comforting or protecting.

I just want the truth.

PROOF OF LIFE

ALL I HAVE to do is go to sleep—quiet my mind, relax my body, and go to sleep. But no matter how I will it, sleep just will not come. My brain is an unfamiliar room and trapdoors are everywhere. Carla's voice loops in my head. *Maybe she never recovered from what happened.* What does that even mean? I look at the clock. 1:00 A.M. Seven hours until Carla comes back. We're going to do some blood tests and send them off to a SCID specialist that I found. Seven hours. I close my eyes. I open them again. 1:01 A.M.

I can't wait for answers to come to me. I have to find them.

It takes all my effort to walk instead of run to my mom's office. I'm sure she's asleep, but I can't risk waking her. I grab the handle and for one horrible moment I think the door will be locked and I will have to wait and I cannot wait. But the handle turns and the room lets me right in like it's been waiting for me, like it's been expecting me.

Her office is perfectly normal, not too neat, not too messy. There are no obvious signs of an unwell mind. Crazy, jumbled, chaotic writings don't cover every inch of the wall.

I walk over to the big desk at the center of the room. It has a built-in file cabinet, so I start there. My hands are shaking, not a tremor, but actual shaking, like an earthquake that only I feel.

My mom is meticulous and extravagant in her record keeping. She's kept everything and it takes me over an hour to get through just a handful of files. There are receipts for big and small purchases, lease agreements, tax documents, warranties, and instruction manuals. She's even kept movie ticket stubs.

Finally, toward the back I find what I'm looking for: a thick red folder labeled *Madeline*. I pull it out carefully and make myself a space on the floor.

The record of my life starts with her pregnancy. I find prenatal vitamin recommendations, sonograms, and photocopies of each visit to the doctor. I find a handwritten index card with two check boxes—one for boy and the other for girl. Girl is checked. My birth certificate is here.

As I search through, it doesn't take me long to realize that I was a sickly baby. I find pediatric sick-visit reports for rashes, allergies, eczema, colds, fevers, and two ear infections, all before I was four months old. I find receipts for lactation and infant-sleep consultants.

When I'm about six months old, just one month after my dad and brother have died, I'm checked into a hospital with Respiratory Syncytial Virus (RSV). I don't know what that is and I make a mental note to google it. It was severe enough to keep me in the hospital for three days.

And then her record keeping becomes less meticulous. I find a printout about RSV from the web. She circled a section that explains that RSV is more severe in people with compromised immune systems. I find a photocopy of the first page of an article on SCID from a medical journal. Her scrawls in the margins are illegible. After that there's a single visit to an allergist and then visits to three different immunologists. Each concludes that no illness was found.

And that's it.

I dig through the cabinet again for more files. It doesn't make sense that this would be all there is. Where are the test results? There must've been a fourth immunologist, right? Where's the diagnosis? Where are the consultations and second opinions? There should be another thick red folder. I scour the files for a third time. And a fourth. I spill other folders to the ground and rifle through them. I hunt through the papers on her desk. I thumb through the pages of her medical journals looking for highlighted passages.

I'm breathing too quickly as I run over to her bookshelves. I pull down books, shake them by their spines willing something to fall out—a forgotten lab result, an official diagnosis. I find nothing.

But nothing is not evidence.

Maybe the proof is elsewhere. It takes me only one try to guess her password—Madeline. I spend two hours looking through every document on her computer. I search her Internet browser history. I look in the trash folder.

Nothing.

Nothing.

Where's the proof of the life I have lived?

I turn a slow pirouette in the middle of the room. I don't

believe the evidence of my own eyes. I don't believe what I'm not seeing. How can there be nothing? It's like my sickness was invented out of the much-too-thin air that I'm breathing.

It's not true. It can't be.

Is it possible that I'm not sick? My mind flinches away from this line of thought.

Maybe she keeps other records in her bedroom? Why didn't I think of that before? 5:23 A.M. Can I wait for her to wake up? No.

The door opens just as I'm walking over to it.

"There you are," she says, relief evident in her voice. "I got worried. You weren't in your room." She comes in farther and her eyes widen as she takes in the chaos surrounding us. "Did we have an earthquake?" she asks. Eventually she realizes the mess is man-made. She turns on me, confused. "Sweetheart, what's going on?"

"Am I sick?" I ask. My blood beats too loudly in my ears.

"What did you say?"

"Am I sick?" I say it louder this time.

Her burgeoning anger dissipates, replaced by concern. "Do you feel sick?"

She reaches out a hand to touch me, but I push it away.

The hurt on her face makes me slightly ill, but I press. "No, that's not what I mean. Do I have SCID?"

Her concern morphs into exasperation and a little pity. "Is this still about that letter?"

"Yes," I say. "And Carla, too. She said that maybe you weren't OK."

"Meaning what?"

What am I accusing her of exactly? "Where are all the papers?" I demand.

She takes a deep breath to steady herself. "Madeline Whittier, what are you talking about?"

"You have records for everything, but there's nothing about SCID in here. Why can't I find anything?" I grab the red folder from the ground and shove it at her. "You have everything else."

"What are you talking about?" she asks. "Of course it's in here."

I'm not sure what I was expecting her to say, but that was not it. Does she really believe it's all here?

She clutches the folder to her chest like she's trying to make it a part of herself. "Did you look carefully? I keep everything."

She walks over to her desk and clears a space. I watch her as she examines the files, rearranging them, smoothing her hands over pages that don't need smoothing.

After a while she looks up at me. "Did you take them? I know they were in here." Her voice is thick with confusion and, also, fear.

And that's when I know for sure.

I am not sick and I never have been.

OUTSIDE

I RUN FROM the office. The hallway stretches out before me and it is endless. I'm in the air lock and it is windless. I'm outside and my breath is soundless.

My heart is beatless.

I vomit all the nothing in my stomach. Bile burns the back of my throat.

I'm crying and the cool morning air chills the tears on my face.

I'm laughing and the cold invades my lungs.

I'm not sick. I've never been sick.

All the emotions I've held in check over the past twenty-four hours crash over me. Hope and despair, anticipation and regret, joy and anger. How is it possible to have an emotion and its opposite at the same time? I'm struggling in a black ocean, a life jacket across my chest, an anchor on my leg.

My mom catches up to me. Her face is a ruin of fear. "What are you doing? What are you doing? You have to get inside."

My vision tunnels and I hold her in my sights. "Why, Mom? Why do I have to go inside?"

"Because you're sick. Bad things could happen to you out here."

She reaches out to me to pull me toward her, but I jerk away from her.

"No. I'm not going back in."

"Please," she begs. "I can't lose you, too. Not after everything."

Her eyes are on me, but I know without a doubt that she's not seeing me at all.

"I lost them. I lost your dad and I lost your brother. I couldn't lose you, too. I just couldn't."

Her face crumbles, falls completely apart. Whatever structures were holding it up give way in a sudden and catastrophic failure.

She's broken. She's been broken for a long time. Carla was right. She never recovered from their deaths.

I say something. I don't know what, but she keeps talking.

"Right after they died you got so, so sick. You wouldn't breathe right and I drove you to the emergency room and we had to stay there for three days. And they didn't know what was wrong. They said it was probably an allergy. They gave me a list of things to stay away from, but I knew it was more than that."

She nods her head. "I knew it was more than that. I had to *protect* you. Anything can happen to you out here."

She looks around. "Anything can happen to you out here. In the world."

I should feel compassion. But that's not what I feel. Anger rises in me and crowds everything else out.

"I'm not sick," I scream. "I've never been sick. You're the one." I stab the air in front of her face. I watch as she shrinks into herself and disappears.

"Come inside," she whispers. "I'll protect you. Stay with me. You're all I have."

Her pain is endless. It falls off the ends of the world.
Her pain is a dead sea.
Her pain is for me, but I cannot bear it anymore.

FAIRY TALES

ONCE UPON A time there was a girl whose entire life was a lie.

THE VOID

A UNIVERSE THAT can wink into existence can wink out again.

BEGINNINGS AND ENDS

FOUR DAYS PASS. I eat. I do homework. I don't read. My mom walks around in a fugue state. I don't think she understands what's happened. She seems to realize that she has something to atone for, but she's not sure exactly what it is. Sometimes she tries to talk to me, but I ignore her. I barely even look at her.

The morning after I realized the truth, Carla took samples of my blood to the SCID specialist, Dr. Chase. We're in his office now, waiting to be called. And even though I know what he'll say, I'm dreading the actual medical confirmation.

Who will I be if I'm not sick?

A nurse calls my name and I ask Carla to stay in the waiting room. For whatever reason, I want to hear this news alone.

Dr. Chase stands when I walk in. He looks just like the photos of him on the Web—older white man with graying hair and bright black eyes.

He looks at me with a mixture of sympathy and curiosity.

He gestures for me to sit, and waits until I do to sit himself.

"Your case," he begins, and then stops.

He's nervous.

"It's OK," I say. "I already know."

He opens a file on his desk, shakes his head like he's still puzzled at the results. "I've gone over these results time and again. I had my colleagues check to be absolutely certain. You're not sick, Ms. Whittier."

He stops and waits for me to react.

I shake my head at him. "I already know," I say again.

"Carla—Nurse Flores—filled me in on your background." He studiously flips through a few more pages, trying to avoid saying what he says next. "As a doctor, your mother would've known this. Granted, SCID is a very rare disease and it comes in many forms, but you have none, absolutely none, of the telltale signs of the disease. If she did any research, any tests at all, she would've known that."

The room falls away and I'm in a featureless white landscape dotted with open doors that lead nowhere.

He's looking at me expectantly when I finally come back to my body. "I'm sorry, did you say something?" I ask.

"Yes. You must have some questions for me."

"Why did I get sick in Hawaii?"

"People get sick, Madeline. Normal, healthy people get sick all the time."

"But my heart stopped."

"Yes. I suspect myocarditis. I spoke with the attending in Hawaii as well. She suspected the same thing. Basically at some point in your past you probably had a viral infection that weakened your heart. Had you been experiencing any chest pain or shortness of breath when you were in Hawaii?"

"Yes," I say slowly, remembering the squeezing of my heart that I'd willfully ignored.

"Well, myocarditis seems like a likely candidate."

I don't have any other questions, not for him anyway. I stand. "Well, thank you very much, Dr. Chase."

He stands, too, agitated and seeming even more nervous than before. "Before you go there's one more thing."

I sit back down. "Because of the circumstance of your upbringing, we're not sure about the state of your immune system."

"What does that mean?"

"We think it's possible that it's underdeveloped, like an infant's."

"An infant?"

"Your immune system hasn't been exposed to a lifetime of common viruses and bacterial infections. It hasn't had time to get experience with fighting these infections. It hasn't had time to get strong."

"So I'm still sick?"

He leans back in his chair. "I don't have a good answer for you. We're in uncharted territory here. I've never heard of a case like this. It may mean that you'll get sick more often than people with healthy immune systems. Or it may mean that when you do get sick, you'll get very severely sick."

"How will I know?"

"I don't think there's any way to know. I recommend caution."

We schedule weekly follow-up visits. He tells me that I should take it slow as I start to see the world—no big crowds, no unfamiliar foods, no exhaustive physical activity.

"The world isn't going anywhere," he says as I leave.

AFTER THE DEATH OF

I SPEND THE next few days searching for more information, for anything that will explain what happened to me and what happened to my mother. I want a diary with her thoughts laid out in legible ink. I want her madness clearly delineated so that I can trace its history and my own. I want details and explanations. I want to know why and why and why. I need to know what happened, but she can't tell me. She's too damaged. And if she could? Would it make a difference? Would I *understand*? Would I understand the depth of grief and fear that could've led her to take my entire life away from me?

Dr. Chase tells me that he thinks she needs a therapist. He thinks it might be a long time before she's able to tell me exactly what happened, if ever. He guesses that she suffered some sort of a breakdown after my dad and brother died.

Carla uses all her persuasive powers trying to convince me not to leave home. Not just for my mom's sake, but for my own. My health is still an unknown.

I consider e-mailing Olly, but so much time has passed. I lied to him. He's probably moved on. He's probably found someone else. I'm not sure I can endure any more heartbreak. And what would I say? I'm almost not sick?

In the end Carla convinces me to stay with my mom. She says I am a better person than that. I'm not so sure. Whoever I was before I found out the truth has died.

ONE WEEK A.D.

I HAVE MY first weekly visit with Dr. Chase. He urges caution.
I install a lock on my bedroom door.

TWO WEEKS A.D.

COMPOSE

INBOX
SENT MAIL
DRAFTS (4)
TRASH
MORE ▼

☐ Madeline, Olly (DRAFT)	I'm sorry, I miss you	Jan 19
☐ Madeline, Olly (DRAFT)	How are you?	Jan 20
☐ Madeline, Olly (DRAFT)	big news	Jan 21
☐ Madeline, Olly (DRAFT)	my mom	Jan 22

THREE WEEKS A.D.

MY MOM TRIES to enter my room, but the door is locked with me in it.

She goes away.

I draft more e-mails to Olly that I don't send.

Dr. Chase continues to urge caution.

FOUR WEEKS A.D.

I PAINT EACH wall in my room a different color. The one by the window is a pale butter yellow. The shelves are sunset orange against a peacock-blue wall. The wall by my headboard is lavender, and the final one is black with chalkboard paint.

My mom knocks on my door, but I pretend not to hear her. She goes away.

FIVE WEEKS A.D.

I ORDER REAL plants for the sunroom. I deprogram the air filters and open the windows. I buy five goldfish and name them all Olly and let them loose in the fountain.

SIX WEEKS A.D.

DR. CHASE INSISTS that it's too soon for me to attempt enrolling in high school. Too many kids with too many illnesses. Carla and I persuade him to let some of my tutors visit in person as long as they're well. He is reluctant, but he agrees.

MADELINE'S MOM

Family Psychiatry Services
33 Bluff Avenue, Santa Monica, CA

Margaret Stevenson
Md., ABPN

2/23/16 4:19 PM
Filed 2/26/16 8:30 PM

Pg 1 of 1

PATIENT
Pauline Whittier (F 51)

ABSTRACT
Patient is finally able to recount the night that her husband and son died. She still speaks of it in the present tense. It's clear we have some work to do.

TRANSCRIPT
Did you know that police officers touch their weapons when they're nervous? It's a tic. I noticed it in the ER, whenever they brought in gang members or robbers. I think touching it calms them. Two of them came to the house after, after it happened. One male, one female. Do they do that on purpose? One male. One female. The female officer did all the talking and she was touching her gun the whole time. She called me ma'am. I think she wanted me to guess her news so she wouldn't have to say it out loud. I'm a doctor. I'm used to giving bad news, but she wasn't. She kept talking. She told me what happened, but I wasn't there anymore. I was back in the nursery with Maddy. I was rubbing her belly. She was sick again. She was always sick. Ear infections. Diarrhea. Bronchitis. The female officer kept talking and I just wanted her to stop. I wanted everything to just stop. No more crying baby, no more sickness, no more hospitals, no more death. If only everything would just stop for once, just stop.

FD: EM

FLOWERS FOR ALGERNON

A WEEK LATER Carla and I watch as Mr. Waterman makes his way across the lawn and to his car to leave. I hugged him before he left. He was surprised, but didn't question it, just hugged me back like it was perfectly natural.

I stay outside for a few minutes after he's left and Carla waits with me. She's trying to find a way to gently break my already broken heart.

"So—" she begins.

I know what she's going to say. She's been gearing up to say it all day. "Please don't leave me, Carla. I still need you."

Her eyes are on me but I can't bear to look at her.

She doesn't deny what I've said, just takes my hand in hers.

"If you really, truly need me to stay, I'll stay." She squeezes my fingers. "But you don't need me."

"I'll always need you." I don't try to stop the tears from coming.

"But not like before," she says gently.

Of course she's right. I don't need her to be here with me for eight hours a day. I don't need constant care. But what will I do without her?

My tears turn into enormous sobs and she holds me in her arms and lets me cry until I reach the end of them.

"What will you do?"

She wipes at my face with the sides of her hands. "I might go back to working in a hospital."

"Did you already tell my mom?"

"This morning."

"What did she say?"

"She thanked me for taking care of you."

I don't try to hide my scowl.

She holds my chin. "When are you going to find it in your heart to forgive her?"

"What she did is not forgivable."

"She was sick, honey. She's still sick."

I shake my head. "She took my whole life away from me." Even now, thinking about all the years I've lost makes me feel like I'm on the lip of an enormous chasm, like I could fall in and never come back out.

Carla nudges me back to the present. "Not your whole life," she says. "You still have a lot left."

We go back inside. I follow her around, watching her pack her things for the last time.

"Did you ever read *Flowers for Algernon*?" I ask.

"Yes."

"Did you like it?"

"No. Not my kind of book. Not enough hope in it."

"It made you cry, didn't it?"

She shakes her head no, but then confesses, "OK, yes, like a baby."

We both laugh.

THE GIFT

A WEEK LATER my mom knocks on my door. I remain where I am on my couch. She knocks again more insistently, and my resentment rises. I'm not sure that our relationship will ever recover. It's hard for me to forgive her when she doesn't fully understand her crime.

I fling open the door as she's about to knock again.

"Now's not a good time," I say.

She flinches, but I don't care. I want to hurt her again and again. My anger is never very far away. I expected it to fade with the passage of time, but it's still right there under the surface of things.

She takes a breath. "I got you something." Her voice is small and confused.

I roll my eyes. "You think presents will help?"

I know I've hurt her again. The present shakes in her hand. I take it because I just want the conversation to be over. I want to lock myself away from her and not have to feel pity or empathy or compassion or anything.

She turns to go but then stops. "I still love you, Madeline. And you still love me. You have your whole life ahead of you. Don't waste it. Forgive me."

THE END IS THE BEGINNING
IS THE END

I OPEN THE present from my mom. It's a phone. It's open to a weather app with the forecast for the week—bright and sunny, every day.

I have to get out of the house. I go outside, not knowing where I'm going until I get there. Fortunately, the ladder is right where Olly left it. I climb up to his roof.

The orrery's still there and still beautiful. The tinfoil suns and moons and stars dangle and twist and reflect the sun's rays back out into the bigger universe. I nudge one of the planets and the entire system rotates slowly. I understand why Olly made it. It's soothing to see an entire world at once—to see the pieces and know how it all fits together.

Was it really just five months ago that I was last up here? It feels like a lifetime ago, like several lifetimes. And the girl that was here? Was that really me? Do I have anything in common with that past Maddy except a strong resemblance and a shared name?

When I was younger one of my favorite activities was imagining alternate-universe versions of myself. Sometimes I was a rosy-cheeked outdoorsy girl who ate flowers and hiked alone, uphill, for miles. Or I was a skydiving, drag-racing, adrenaline-fueled daredevil. Or a chain mail–wearing, sword-swinging dragon slayer. It was fun to imagine those things because I already knew who I was. Now I don't know anything. I don't know who I'm supposed to be in my new world.

I keep trying to pinpoint the moment when everything changed. The moment that set my life on this path. Was it when my dad and brother died, or was it before that? Was it when they first got into the car on the day they died? Was it when my brother was born? Or when my mom and dad met? Or when my mom was born? Maybe it was none of those. Maybe it was when the truck driver decided he wasn't too tired to drive. Or when he decided to become a truck driver in the first place. Or when he was born.

Or any of the infinite number of moments that led to this one.

So, if I could change one moment, which one would I pick? And would I get the results I want? Would I still be Maddy? Would I have lived in this house? Would a boy named Olly have moved in next door? Would we have fallen in love?

Chaos theory says that even a small change in initial conditions can lead to wildly unpredictable results. A butterfly flaps her wings now and a hurricane forms in the future.

Still.

I think if I could just find the moment, I could take it apart piece by piece, molecule by molecule, until I got down to the atomic level, until I got to the part that was inviolate and essential. If I could take it apart and understand it then maybe I could make just exactly the right change.

I could fix my mom and make it so she was never broken.

I could understand how I came to be sitting on this roof at the beginning and at the end of everything.

FUTURE PERFECT #2

☒ ✉ ☒ ☒ ☒ ☒

From: Madeline F. Whittier
To: genericuser033@gmail.com
Subject: Future Perfect #2
Sent: March 10, 7:33 PM

By the time you read this you will have forgiven me.

TAKEOFF

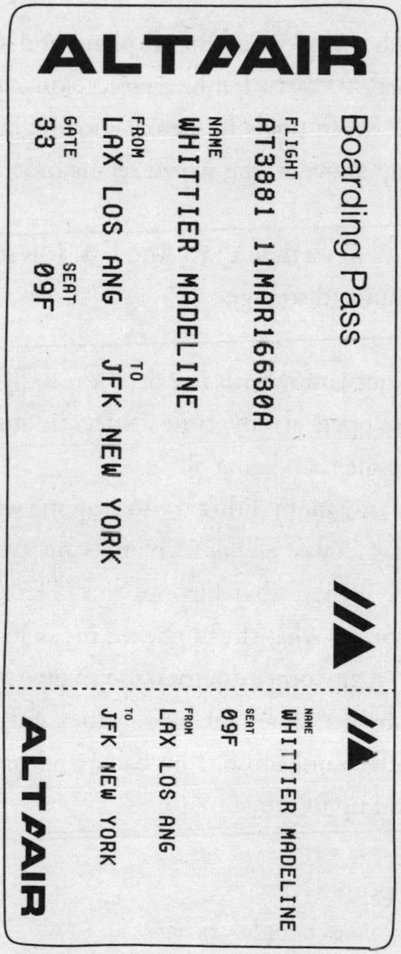

ALTAIR

Boarding Pass

FLIGHT
AT3881 11MAR16630A

NAME
WHITTIER MADELINE

FROM
LAX LOS ANG

TO
JFK NEW YORK

GATE
33

SEAT
09F

///▶

NAME
WHITTIER MADELINE

SEAT
09F

FROM
LAX LOS ANG

TO
JFK NEW YORK

///▶

ALTAIR

299

FORGIVENESS

I STARE OUT the window of the airplane and see miles and miles of greenery sectioned into perfect squares. Dozens of mysterious blue-green pools lie below, glowing at their edges. From so high up above it, the world seems ordered and deliberate.

But I know it's more than that. And less. It is structured and chaotic. Beautiful and strange.

Dr. Chase was not happy with my decision to fly so soon. But anything can happen at any time. Safety is not everything. There's more to life than being alive.

To her credit, my mom didn't try to stop me when I told her last night. She swallowed all her fear and panic even though she still doesn't fully believe that I'm not sick. Her doctor's brain struggles to reconcile what she's believed for so long against the evidence of too many other doctors, too many tests. I'm trying to put myself in her shoes, playing games not of cause and effect, but of effect and cause. I go back, and back, and back, and I always end up in the same place.

Love.

Love makes people crazy.

Loss of love makes people crazy.

My mother loved my father. He was the love of her life. And she loved my brother. He was the love of her life. And she loves me. I am the love of her life.

The universe took my dad and brother away. For her it was the Big Bang in reverse—everything that became a nothing.

I can understand that.

Almost.

I am trying to.

"When will you come back home?" she asked.

And I told her the truth. "I don't know if this is home anymore."

She cried then, but still she let me go, and that has to count for something.

Eventually the cloud cover grows too thick for me to see much of anything. I relax into my seat and reread *The Little Prince*. And, just like every time I've read it before, the meaning changes.

LIFE IS SHORT™

SPOILER REVIEWS BY MADELINE

THE LITTLE PRINCE BY ANTOINE DE SAINT-EXUPÉRY

Spoiler alert: Love is worth everything. Everything.

THIS LIFE

EVEN AT 9 A.M. on a Saturday, New York City is just as loud and jam-packed as it's famous for being. The streets are filled with honking, slow-moving cars. The sidewalks teem with people just narrowly missing each other, as if their movements were choreographed. From the back of the cab I let the noise and smells of the city wash over me. I open my eyes wide to take in all the world I see.

I didn't tell Olly what I was up to, just that there was a present waiting for him at a used book-store close to his house. I imagined our reunion for almost the entire flight. Every scenario involved us kissing within the first thirty seconds.

The driver drops me off outside of Ye Olde Book Shoppe. I push through the doors. Right away I know that I will eventually spend a lot of time here.

The store is a small single room with floor-to-ceiling shelves, each overflowing with books. The room is dimly lit by small penlights attached to each shelf so that books are just about all you see. The air smells like nothing I've ever imagined. It smells *old*. As if it has been in this same place for a very long time.

I have fifteen minutes before Olly will be here. I wander the aisles gawking at all the books. I want to touch them all at once. I want to add my name to all the people who read them before me. I trace my fingers across the spines. Some are so worn, so well used, that I can barely make out the titles.

I check the time on my phone. It's almost time. I make my way to the end of the S–U aisle and hide. My butterflies have come back.

A minute later, I watch as he walks slowly down the aisle examining the shelves.

His hair has grown in. He has big floppy curls that soften the angles of his face. Also, he's not wearing all black. Well, his jeans and sneakers are black, but his T-shirt is gray. And I think he's taller somehow.

More than anything I've experienced in the last few weeks—saying good-bye to Carla, leaving home against Dr. Chase's advice, leaving my mom in her sadness—seeing him looking so different causes me the most panic.

I don't know why I expected him to be the same. *I'm* not.

He takes out his phone to read my instructions again.

•••••○   10:12 AM

◀   Olly

6:44 AM
Madeline Whittier

There's a present waiting for you

10:00AM. Ye Olde Book Shoppe

Aisle S-U

You'll know it when you see it

📷 [   ] Send

He slips the phone into his pocket and looks back at the shelves. I placed the book, cover facing out, in front of all the others so he'd be sure not to miss it. He doesn't. But instead of picking it up, he slips his hands into his pockets and stares.

A few days ago, when I was communing with the orrery, I was trying so hard to find the single pivotal moment that set my life on its path. The moment that answered the question, *How did I get here?*

But it's never just one moment. It's a series of them. And your life can branch out from each one in a thousand different ways. Maybe there's a version of your life for all the choices you make and all the choices you don't.

Maybe there's a version of my life where I'm sick after all.

A version where I die in Hawaii.

Still another where my father and brother are still alive and my mother is not broken.

There's even a version of my life without Olly in it.

But not this one.

Olly pulls his hands out of his pockets, plucks the book from the shelf and reads. He grins and bounces lightly on the balls of his feet.

I come out of hiding. I walk down the aisle toward him.

The smile he gives me is worth living for.

"Found your book," he says.

→ REWARD IF FOUND:

- ~~Snorkel with me (Madeline) off Molokini to spot the Hawaiian~~
  ~~state fish — the Humuhumunukunukuapua'a.~~

- ~~A visit with me (Madeline) to a used-book store.~~

- Me (Madeline).

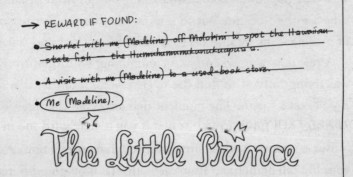

The Little Prince

WRITTEN AND ILLUSTRATED BY

ANTOINE DE SAINT-EXUPÉRY

TRANSLATED FROM THE FRENCH BY RICHARD HOWARD

A HARVEST BOOK
HARCOURT, INC.

Orlando   New York   San Diego   Toronto   London

ACKNOWLEDGMENTS

YOU ARE TRULY a thorough reader if you're here with me in the acknowledgments. And, as a truly thorough reader of books (and their acknowledgments), you know that books do not spring wholly formed from the addled minds of their authors.

First, I'd like to thank my mom, who has always dreamed big enough for the both of us. No, Oprah hasn't selected me for her book club yet, Mom. But! It could happen.

When I was young and growing up in Jamaica, my dad wrote movie reviews for a local paper. I thought that it (writing) and him (my dad) were just the coolest. So. I have to thank my dad for showing me that you could write things on paper that came from your head and that those things could affect people.

I need to thank the Thursday night drinking and writing crew from Emerson College. You know who you are. You guys were my first community of writers and what a talented, crazy, supportive, mostly sober group you were. In particular, I need to thank Wendy Wunder. You are generous and funny and one of the best writers I know.

Thanks to Joelle Hobeika, Sara Shandler, Natalie Sousa, and Josh Bank at Alloy. You made the book better in every way. I especially want to thank Sara for being a mad scientist genius and

Joelle (also a genius) for making me laugh and feel good even when giving me twelve pages of single-spaced, double-sided revision notes.

And then there's Wendy Loggia. Truly, I won the lottery having you as my editor. Thank you for your vision and passion and kindness. You believed in this book from the very first words and that has meant the world to me. Another huge thanks to my tireless publicist, Jillian Vandall, and then to the entire team at Delacorte for making my biggest, oldest, wildest dream come true.

Finally to my husband, David Yoon. Thank you for drawing me beautiful things at 4 A.M. in between kisses and sips of coffee. Thank you for everything, everything. For love. For adventure. For family. For this life. I love you.

Get ready to fall for Natasha and Daniel
on the single day that will change
both of their lives forever . . .

NEW YORK TIMES BESTSELLING AUTHOR OF
EVERYTHING, EVERYTHING

THE
SUN IS
ALSO A
STAR

nicola yoon

Turn over to read an exclusive preview.

natasha

RED TIE LOOKS AWAY FROM ME. I think he's about to cry, which makes no sense at all. He offers to buy me new headphones. Even if I let him, new ones couldn't replace these.

I've had them since right after we moved to America. When my father bought them for me, he was still hopeful for all he would accomplish here. He was still trying to convince my mom that the move away from the country of our birth, away from all our friends and family, would be worth it in the end. He was going to hit it big. He was going to get the American Dream that even Americans dream about.

He used me and my brother to help convince my mom. He bought us gifts on layaway, things we could barely afford even on layaway. If we were happy here, then maybe the move was right after all.

I didn't care what the reason for the gifts was. These way-too-expensive headphones were my favorite of them all. I only cared that they were my favorite color and promised audiophile-quality sound. They were my first love. They know all my secrets. They know how much I used to worship my dad.

They know that I kind of hate myself for not worshiping him at all now.

It seems like such a long time ago when I thought the world of him. He was some exotic planet and I was his favorite satellite. But he's no planet, just the final fading light of an already dead star.

And I'm not a satellite. I'm space junk, hurtling as far as I can away from him.

daniel

I DON'T THINK I'VE EVER noticed anyone the way I'm noticing her. Sunlight filters through her hair, making it look like a kind of halo around her head. A thousand emotions pass over her face. Her eyes are black and wide, with long lashes. I can imagine staring into them for a long time. Right now they're dull, but I know exactly what they would look like bright and laughing. I wonder if I can make her laugh. Her skin is a warm and glowing brown. Her lips are pink and full, and I'm probably staring at them for far too long. Fortunately, she's too sad to notice what a shallow (and horny) jerk I am.

She looks up from her broken headphones. As our eyes meet, I get a kind of déjà vu, but instead of feeling like I'm repeating something in the past, it feels like I'm experiencing something that will happen in my future. I see us in old age. I can't see our faces; I don't know where or even when we are. But I have a strange and happy feeling that I can't quite describe. It's like knowing all the words to a song but still finding them beautiful and surprising.

natasha

I STAND UP AND DUST myself off. This day can't get any worse. It must eventually end. "Were you following me?" I ask him. I'm crankier and testier than I should be with someone who just saved my life.

"Man, I knew you would think that."

"You just happened to be right behind me?" I fiddle with my headphones, trying to reattach the ear pad, but it's hopeless.

"Maybe I was meant to save your life today," he says.

I ignore that. "Okay, thanks for your help," I say, preparing to leave.

"At least tell me your name," he blurts out.

"Red Tie—"

"Daniel."

"Okay, Daniel. Thank you for saving me."

"That's a long name." His eyes don't leave mine. He's not going to give up until I tell him.

"Natasha."

I think he's going to shake my hand again, but instead he shoves his hands into his pockets. "Nice name."

"So glad you approve," I say, giving him my most sarcastic tone.

He doesn't say anything else, just looks at me with a slight frown, as if he's trying to figure something out.

Finally I can't take it anymore. "Why are you staring at me?"

He blushes again, and now I'm staring. I can see how it might be fun to tease him just to get him to blush. I let my eyes wander the sharp planes of his face. He is classically handsome; debonair, even. Watching him stand there in his suit, I can picture him in a black-and-white Hollywood romantic comedy trading witty banter with his heroine. His eyes are clear brown and deep-set. Somehow I can tell he smiles a lot. His thick black hair is pulled back into a ponytail.

Observable Fact: The ponytail pushes him from handsome to kind of sexy.

"Now *you're* staring," he says to me. It's my turn to blush.

I clear my throat. "Why are you wearing a suit?"

"I have an interview later. Wanna go get something to eat?"

"What for?" I ask.

"Yale. Alumni admission interview. I applied early decision."

I shake my head. "No, I meant why do you want to get something to eat?"

"I'm hungry?" he says, as if he's not sure exactly.

"Hmmm," I say. "I'm not."

"Coffee, then? Or tea or soda or filtered water?"

"Why?" I ask, realizing that he's not going to give up.

His shoulders shrug, but his eyes don't. "Why not? Besides, I'm pretty sure you owe me your life since I just saved it."

"Believe me," I tell him, "you don't want my life."

NICOLA YOON grew up in Jamaica (the island) and Brooklyn (part of Long Island). She currently resides in Los Angeles with her husband and daughter, both of whom she loves beyond all reason. *Everything, Everything* is her first novel. Her second is entitled *The Sun Is Also a Star*.

DAVID YOON is a writer and designer. He lives with his wife Nicola Yoon (see above) in Los Angeles, where they spend their days talking about stories and reading to their three-year-old daughter, Penny. David created the illustrations for *Everything, Everything*.